ISBN 978-1-333-77565-0
PIBN 10546531

HISTORICAL, GENEALOGICAL, AND BIOGRAPHICAL ACCOUNT

OF THE

JOLLIFFE FAMILY

OF VIRGINIA,

1652 to 1893.

ALSO

SKETCHES OF THE NEILL'S, JANNEY'S, HOLLINGSWORTH'S, AND OTHER COGNATE FAMILIES.

PHILADELPHIA:
PRINTED BY J. B. LIPPINCOTT COMPANY.
1893.

GUTEKUNST

FREE GRAMMAR SCHOOL. STRATFORD-ON-AVON.

HISTORICAL, GENEALOGICAL, AND BIOGRAPHICAL ACCOUNT

OF THE

JOLLIFFE FAMILY

OF VIRGINIA,

1652 to 1893.

ALSO

SKETCHES OF THE NEILL'S, JANNEY'S, HOLLINGSWORTH'S, AND OTHER COGNATE FAMILIES.

PHILADELPHIA:
PRINTED BY J. B. LIPPINCOTT COMPANY.
1893.

One Hundred and Fifty Copies Printed.

No...............................

"It is a useful employment for societies, as well as individuals, to look back through their past history and mark the dealings of a kind Providence toward them." (Bishop Meade.) "It is wise for us to recur to the history of our ancestors. Those who are regardless of their ancestors, and of their posterity, who do not look upon themselves as a link connecting the past with the future in the transmission of life from their ancestors to their posterity, do not perform their duty to the world. To be faithful to ourselves we must keep our ancestors and posterity within reach and grasp of our thoughts and affections. *L*iving in the memory and retrospect of the past, and hoping with affection and care for those who are to come after us, we are true to ourselves only when we act with becoming pride for the blood we inherit, and which we are to transmit to those who shall fill our places." (Daniel Webster.) "I have never known a person whose self-reliance was of so austere a cast that he did not take pleasure when it was in his power to do so in tracing his descent from an honored line." (Edward Everett.)

PREFACE.

WHILE living in Philadelphia in the year 1870 I had occasion to hunt up some dates relating to older members of our family. I found the search by no means an easy one; for by the burning of the old homestead soon after the late war a great number of valuable papers, letters, and books were destroyed. These referred especially to my father's family, as the homestead was owned by my great-uncle, who was the eldest son and inherited most of the landed property, and with it also the old Revolutionary papers of his father, Captain John Jolliffe. I regret the loss of these exceedingly, as they covered such a very interesting period. Some of them, relating to lands which this ancestor received for Revolutionary services, were in the hands of a lawyer in Winchester, and were taken, with the Court archives, somewhere up the valley, to save them from destruction by soldiers or camp-followers during the late war. The archives, even to the first old deed-book, have fortunately been restored, but all efforts to recover our papers have thus far been unavailing, although the deed to this land has come back to us in a curious and roundabout way. Happily, this ancestor, before he joined the fray of 1776, stepped from a peaceful line, whose records up to a certain date are safely laid away in the Meeting Records at Hopewell, Virginia. Before this friendly period I had the Court-House records and the General Land Office at Richmond to fall back upon.

Thus the difficulties in my path but added interest to my search, which was continued from time to time, when I had the leisure, in desultory fashion. In late years, however, I have taken up the subject seriously and systematically, and what was begun as a pastime has proved a great blessing in helping me through many invalid hours. A little over a year since, in looking through these data with a relative, it was suggested that I publish them for the benefit of my children and those of the family who might be interested. Hence these imperfect pages, which were never intended for the public eye.

It is probably safe to say that no genealogy of a large family has ever been written without some mistakes, and this book will probably form no exception to the general rule, although I have carefully endeavored to make no statements positively without having the best of authority therefor. My researches have involved much time, labor, and expense, spread out as they have been, necessarily, over a large territory, especially in the South, where the genealogist finds no royal road cast up for him in the way of carefully preserved records gathered into the many historical societies that are scattered all over New England and the Eastern States.

My sources of information have been various. The libraries of Philadelphia, Baltimore, Washington, and Richmond have yielded me much valuable information, also family Bibles and papers, Friends' Meeting records of Bucks County, Pennsylvania, Chester County, Pennsylvania, of Maryland and Virginia, especially those of East Nottingham, Maryland, Hopewell and Fairfax, Virginia, and Church records of various denominations in Virginia. The General Land Office at Richmond, Virginia, has aided me greatly in information about our earliest ancestors that otherwise would have been impossible to obtain. There I found copies of the original patents of land they took up under the Crown and Lord Fairfax, some of which I have given in these pages, as they are quaintly and curiously worded. There, too, are the proceedings of the General Assembly relative to military grants and copies of the general warrants to Virginia officers during the Revolution, some of which I have also given. The various Court records also have been examined, especially those of Norfolk County, at Portsmouth, Virginia, and of Frederick County, at Winchester, Virginia. Relatives and friends have also aided with books, old letters, and personal information.

No effort to carry this research, with regard to the families mentioned, into England or Ireland has been attempted, and the information given has only been such as has been obtained from family records and such English works as are to be found in our public libraries. The Rush Library, in Philadelphia, is especially rich in such volumes. I have been very careful to give my authorities for what I have published on this subject, and owing to limited space have had to omit much that was very interesting. It may, however, furnish a starting-point for some member of the family to finish what I have begun.

In order not to confuse the reader, an effort has been made to keep the generations distinct. Wherever a date is given and not qualified, it has been copied from a reliable record, such as a Family Bible, Meeting or Court-House record. When the record does not give the exact date, and it is gathered from contemporaneous records, circumstances, etc., it is given as about such and such a time.

Having commenced my title-page with a sentiment from good old Bishop Meade, that "it is wise for us to look back through the past history of our ancestors and mark the dealings of a kind Providence towards them," I found the wisdom of this remark constantly brought before my mind in the compilation of the following pages. I have found, though not always among the great of the earth, so many in all the generations have been among the good, not only proving their faith by their works, but often sealing it by suffering therefor. If my own children or any of my young relatives should catch an inspiration from the simple record of their adherence to duty, often amid trying circumstances, the labor that I have put upon these pages will not have been spent in vain.

"Knowing this—that never yet
Share of truth was vainly set
In the world's wide fallow;
After hands shall sow the seed,
After hands from hill and mead
Reap the harvest yellow."

WHITTIER.

WILLIAM JOLLIFFE.

BRANHAM, VIRGINIA,
June 23, 1893.

ANTIQUITY AND HISTORICAL NOTES OF THE ENGLISH ANCESTRY OF THE JOLLIFFE FAMILY.

THAT portion of the west of England embracing that remarkable tier of counties, namely, Lancastershire, Cheshire, Staffordshire, and Worcestershire, though small in extent, is one of the most densely populated in the world, and green fields appear almost obliterated by the masses of brickwork raised by human hands. Lancastershire and Cheshire include within their borders the basins of the Mersey and the Ribble, and here are carried on the most extensive mining and manufacturing works in the world. Worcestershire occupies the central portion of the fertile valley of the Severn. The Teme, which comes down from the Welsh hills, flows through a narrow valley, while the Avon irrigates the fertile vale of Eversham. Staffordshire lies wholly within the great central plain of England. The river Trent rises near the northern boundary of the county, and passes through its centre, receiving on its way several tributaries, the principal of which are the Dove on the east and the Tame on the west. This Trent valley is noted for its fertility, but Staffordshire is essentially a manufacturing and mining county. The northern portion of the county is known as the potteries, for the manufacture of earthenware has been carried on there from times out of mind. The southern portion of the county is the great coal-mining district known as the "Black Country." Lying between these two districts is to be found in the valley of the Dove one of the most beautiful and picturesque spots in all England. The Churnet is tributary to the Dove and hardly yields to it in romantic beauty. Near the source of the Churnet is to be found the considerable town of Leek, where silk is extensively manufactured. "This town of Leek and the surrounding country once belonged to Algar of Mercia, and at the Conquest was given to Hugh Lupus, first earl of Chester. Ralph, the sixth earl, gave it to Dieulacresse Abbey, which he founded in the thirteenth century. The old church is dedicated to St. Edward the Confessor. This church was burned down in 1279 and was rebuilt. It is noted for its beautiful rose window" "One mile north of the town is Dieulacresse Abbey, founded in 1214 for the Cistercians by Ralph de Blondeville, sixth earl of Chester. He was a renowned crusader and liberal to all monastic orders. It was granted by Edward the Sixth to Sir Ralph Bagenal, and by him was pulled down and the present farm-house erected." Careswell, sometimes called Caverswell, is three miles west of the town of Cheadle, and one and one-half miles north of Leek. It has a small population. "The church has a monument by Chantry to Lady St. Vincent, and another to Sir William Caverswell, the builder of the castle (Temp. Edward I., 1275), which is styled by Leland 'the prati pile of Careswell.' It seems to have fallen into ruin, and in 1643 Matthew Craddock built the present castle. It was for some time occupied by a community of nuns, and there is a Roman Catholic church in the grounds."

This region is rendered doubly interesting to us because it was here that the family of Jolli, or Jolliffe, settled and lived for many years after the Norman Conquest. They were located at Leek, Coften Hacketts, Bothoms, Careswell, and Dieulacresse (Staffordshire); Bromsgrove (Cheshire); Buglawton, Upton-Snodesbury, Cofton Hall, and Worcester (Worcestershire); Hayton Castle (Lancastershire); Typed-Magdalen, Stower-Preaux, Stower-Estower (Dorsetshire); Stratford-on-the-Avon, and in London. "Towards the latter end of the reign of Edward the Second, Sir William de Careswell built a large and uncommonly strong stone castle at this place, and surrounded it by extensive ponds and a deep moat, with a drawbridge. The heads of the ponds had square turrets. It was for a long time the chief seat of the long and ancient family of the Vanes, now extinct." (Worcester Antiquities.) "Careswell was Twentieth Conqueror, held of Robert de Stafford, by Ernulph de Hesding. In the reign of Richard the First, one Thomas de Careswell, Knt., whose grandson, William de Careswell, erected a goodly castle in this place, the pools, dams, and houses of office being all of masonry. His posterity enjoyed it until the 19th of Edward the Third, when by heir general it passed from the Careswells to the Montgomerys, and from them, by the Giffords and the Ports, to the family of Hastings, Earls of Huntingdon, who were the owners in the 17th century. In 1655 Matthew Craddock owned it.[1] From the Craddocks it passed to the Vanes. Thus William Viscount Vane of Ireland, who possessed it in right of his mother, the daughter and co-heir of Sir William Jolliffe, Knt., who married Mary, daughter of Ferdinando, the Sixth Earl of Huntingdon." (T. R. Nash's History of Worcestershire.)

"Dieulacresse Monastery was in possession of —— Jolli of Leek

[1] In 1655 this property belonged to Thomas Jolliffe, who was an officer of Charles I., and attended him to his execution. His property was forced to a sale, and Matthew Craddock bought it.

prior to 1637, when it appears to have been held by Sir Benjamin Rudyard." (Dugdale.) "At Leek are eight almshouses, endowed in 1696 by Elizabeth, widow, and eldest daughter of William Jolliffe, of this place, for eight poor widows, who are allowed two shillings per week, and seven shillings 5 pense and 3 farthings twice a year for coals, and a new gown once in two years." (Shaw's Staffordshire.) "In Bentley-Meere Church tables of benefaction for the poor hang up in the church. Mr. Marmaduke Jolly bequeathed ten pounds, the interest to be annually applied to the teaching of poor children at Bentley school. This is paid by the church wardens." "The name of Jolliffe, old English Jollif, French Joli, is translated as jolly, gay, trim, fine, gallant, neat, handsome, etc." "Up ryst this jolyf lover Absalom." (Chaucer, 3688.) "In all works of family history the name seems to have originally been spelled Jolli or Jolly, and is of French or Norman origin." "The family of Jolliffe (originally Jolli) is of considerable antiquity in the counties of Stafford and Worcester, and the pedigree in possession of the senior members comprises intermarriages with many eminent and noble houses. One branch, established in the north, enjoyed, it appears from authentic records, power and affluence even before the institution in Europe of hereditary honors." (Burke's Landed Gentry of Great Britain.) Another account says, "Descended from an ancient and honorable family which dates its origin from the incursion of the Norman Conqueror, and collaterally allied to some of the chief nobles of the kingdom." As a family they seem to have been home lovers, clinging closely to the place of their nativity, adhering to old customs and the existing order of things with great tenacity, and not easily influenced to adopt either new forms of religion or government. They were not, nor ever have been, what might be called a restless people. They were a tall, dark-haired and blue-eyed race, not an uncommon type of people found in the west of England of Norman extraction, as shown by various printed records still extant. During the troublous times of Charles the First and the Cromwell revolution they were stanch royalists, and adherents of the Established Church, one of them attending Charles to the place of execution. For their loyalty and religious convictions they were made to suffer, as Cromwell and his followers knew only too well how to create suffering by depriving them of all rank, position, and estates. Macaulay says, "Charles relied, indeed, chiefly for pecuniary aid on the munificence of his adherents. Many of these mortgaged their lands, pawned their jewels, broke up their silver chargers and christening bowls in order to assist him. When the struggle was over, the work of innovation and revenge was pushed on with ardor; the clashing polity of the kingdom was remodelled; most of the old clergy were ejected from their benefices; fines, often of ruinous amounts, were laid on the royalists, already impoverished by large aids furnished to the king. Many estates were confiscated, many proscribed cavaliers found it expedient to purchase, at an enormous cost, the protection of eminent members of the victorious party. Large domains, belonging to the Crown, to the Bishops, and to the Chapters, were seized, and either granted away or put up to auction. In consequence of these spoliations a great part of the soil of England was at once offered for sale; as money was scarce, as the market was glutted, and the title was insecure, and as the awe inspired by power always prevented free competition, the prices were often merely nominal. Thus many old and honorable families disappeared and were heard of no more, and many a new man rose rapidly to affluence." At the Restoration their property was restored to them, and they were reinstated to the royal favor. They furnished from their number magistrates and sheriffs of the counties of Stafford and Worcester during the reigns of Charles the First and Charles the Second, William and Annie, and George the Second. They have been aldermen and lord mayors of the city of London, members of Parliament, and governors of provinces. Many of them were men of note as authors, physicians, soldiers, and, above all, as philanthropists. The arms borne by the English family are "Argent on a pile Azure, three Dexter Gauntlets of the Field. The crest, a Cubit arm erect vested and cuffed, the sleeve charged with a pile Argent, the hand grasping a sword ppd." The motto, "Tant que je puis."

THE JOLLIFFE FAMILY OF ENGLAND.

15

1. JOHN JOLLIE, living about the middle of the sixteenth century, married "Margaret, daughter of Ranchey." Their first son died without issue; their second son was Thomas Jollie, 2, of Leek, in the county of Stafford, and of Buglawton, in Cheshire, who married (first) Margaret, daughter of Laurence Swettenham, of Someford, county of Chester. They had a son, William Jollie, born in 1574, of Bothoms, in Staffordshire; and a son, Thomas Jollie, of Leek, in the county of Stafford, who was lord mayor of London in 1615, whose son was Sir John Jolliffe, of London.

"Laurence Swettenham, age 18, the 29th of Henry the Eighth (1538), died 21st of Elizabeth (1579), when not forty years of age. (A mistake of 18 years.) Will was probated Jan. 1597–8. His wife was Elisabeth, daughter and heiress of John Oldfield, of Sutton, near Macclesfield. His children were Edmund, Anthony, Annie, Elizabeth, Jane, Margaret, Mary, Katherine, Alice, Frances, Eleanor, Margery, and Ursula. He was a man of prominence." "Sir William Jolliffe (son of William of Bothoms) married Mary, daughter of Ferdinando, the sixth earl of Huntington. They left one daughter and heir, Mary, who married Viscount Vane of Ireland, through whom the Jolliffes acquired Careswell Castle." "In Careswell Church is a monument, erected to the memory of William de Careswell, the builder of the castle. It bears the following inscription 'Wilhelmus de Careswellus.' This is at the head; surrounding it is this distich in Latin, which, when Anglicized, reads:

'I built this castle with its rampiers round
For the use of the living, who are under ground.'

"The following lines have since been added,—namely·

'William of Careswell, here lye I,
That built this castle and the pools here by;
William of Careswell, here thou mayest lye;
But thy Castle is down and thy pools are dry.'"

(Worcester Antiquities.)

3. William Jollie of Bothoms, parish of Chedleton, in Staffordshire, wedded Annie, daughter of Benedict Webb of Kingwood, in Gloucestershire. They had a son, Thomas Jollie, or Jolliffe, of Crofton Hall, in the county of Worcester; a son, William Jolliffe,

of Careswell Castle, Staffordshire (this was Sir William, who married Mary, daughter of the Earl of Huntingdon); a daughter, Elizabeth, who married Roland Hill, Esquire, of Hawkstone, Shropshire (he was father of the celebrated Roland Hill, who suffered during the Civil Wars, who was the father of Sir Richard Hill, a noted diplomat of Queen Anne's time (T. R. Nash); and probably other children. He died June 11, 1669, aged eighty-five years.

"Ashcomb is built upon the site of an old manor house, formerly called Bottom Hall, belonging to the Jolliffes, who had half the Manor, and a very extensive estate in this parish (which is that of Chedleton, belonging to Alstonfield) and the adjoining parishes." "Mary Hastings, wife of William Jolliffe of Careswell Castle, County of Stafford, died December 4th, 1678, and is buried in St. Martin's-in-the-Fields." (Collectanea Topographica, etc.) "This William (of Bothams) had a son, Sir William. He died in 1669. In Richard Baxter's will he was appointed to invest two hundred pounds in real estate." (Athenæ Cantabrigienses.) "Phillip Papillon of Acrise (M.P. for Dover), Kent County, borne in 1660, married 1689 Annie, daughter of William Jolliffe, Esquire, of Bothoms, by whom he had an only son David." "Sir Samuel Moyer, Bart., of Low-Leyton, in Essex, England, was High Sheriff of Essex in 1698; he had also been one of the counsel of State. His widow, Lady Rebecca Jolliffe Moyer, was a daughter of Sir William Jolliffe, Bart., and she founded the well-known 'Lady Moyer's Lectures.'" (Diary of Samuel Pepys, in 1667.)

4. Thomas Jollie, or Jolliffe, Esquire, of Cofton Hall, in the county of Worcester, wedded (first) Margaret, daughter and co-heir of Richard Skinner of Cofton (by Margaret, daughter of Sir Edward Littleton, Knt., of Pillaton, and Margaret, his wife, daughter and co-heir of Sir William Devereux, son of Walter, Viscount Hereford[1]), by whom he left issue five sons and two daughters (she died January 6, 1647, aged twenty-seven years and two months):

---

[1] This Walter, Viscount Hereford, was the celebrated Walter Devereux, first Earl of Essex of his name. He succeeded his grandfather in the title of Viscount Hereford, and recommended himself to Queen Elizabeth by his bravery in suppressing the rebellion of the Earls of Northumberland and Westmoreland in 1569. For this service he was given the Garter and the Earldom of Essex. He was opposed to the great O'Neill in Ireland, and was obliged to sue for peace and required to give up his command just as he had almost expelled the invading Scots from the western islands of his territory. Promises made by the Queen to him were but poorly kept; he was overcome with grief, which brought on a fatal disease. His countess soon after married the Earl of Leicester. He was the

(1) William Jolliffe, ob. cœlebs, æt. thirteen.
(2) Thomas Jolliffe, ob. cœlebs, æt. seventeen.
(3) John Jolliffe, ob sine prole (the American heir).
(4) Benjamin Jolliffe (his heir).
(5) Annie Jolliffe (married to Alexander Felton, of Ganesworth, in Cheshire).
(6) Margaret Jolliffe (married Filson Bruin, of Stapleford, Cheshire);

and a son whose name is not recorded.

Thomas married (second) Mary, daughter of Sir Gabriel Lowe, Knt., of Newark, county of Gloucester, and by that lady (who died in 1663) left a son, William Jolliffe, obiit cœlebs aput, London, March 6, 1680, æt. twenty-three. Thomas Jolliffe was a justice of the peace, and died October 23, 1693, aged seventy-six years.

I now leave the main line in order to properly explain an intermarriage; it therefore becomes necessary for me to go back to the second generation and give the following brief narrative:

2. Thomas Jollie, of Leek (the second son of the first Thomas, of Leek), was born about the year 1585 or 1586. He was lord mayor of London, 1615. His wife was Elizabeth, daughter of Edward Mainwaring, Esq., of Whitmore. His son John, of London, whose wife was Rebecca, daughter of Walter Boothby, Esq., was one of the aldermen of the city; he had a son, Sir William Jolliffe (his wife, Mary Hastings, died December 4, 1678, and was buried in St. Martin's-in-the-Fields), whose daughter was Lady Rebecca Jolliffe, who married Sir Samuel Moyer, Bart., of Lower-Leyton, Essex. John Jollie, of London (Sir John Jolles, London, July 23, 1606), had a daughter Elizabeth, who married John Tufnaile, of London, and Monkin Hadley, Middlesex County. William Tufnaile assumed the surname of Jolliffe, pursuant to a will of Sir William Jolliffe, and died April 21, 1797. The Tufnailes owned the estate of New Monc-

---

father of Robert II., Earl of Essex, the favorite of Queen Elizabeth, and grandfather of the Earl of Essex who led the Parliament forces against Charles I. He was the great-great-grandfather of the mother of the immigrant John Jolliffe. "Sir Charles *L*ittleton of Sheene, Worcester, brother of Sir Henry *L*ittleton, of Worcestershire, who had a great estate, had no children. Descendant of the great lawyer of that name; same arms and motto. Married Mrs. Temple, one of the late Queen's maids."

ton, in Yorkshire, inherited in 1796 from William Tufnaile Jolliffe. Their arms: "Argent on a Pile Vert, three dexter hands coupd at the wrist, and erected of the First, is borne by the name of Jollye, and was confirmed unto William Jollye of Leek, in the county of Stafford, son of John Jollye of Leek aforesaid, who was son of John Jollye of the same place by ——, the 27th of August, 1614, in the 12th year of the reign of King James the First." "He beareth Argent on a Pile Azure, three dexter Gauntlets of the Field, by the name Jolliffe; and is the coat armour of John Jolliffe of the City of London, Esquire, Governor of the Muscovy Company, descended from the family of the Jolliffes of Botham, in Staffordshire. 'This coat is also borne by William Jolliffe of Careswell Castle, in Staffordshire.'" "Coston, or Coston Hackett, in the county of Worcester, was so called from Hoar Stone, or Whorstone." "In 1680, at St. Michaels, Barbadoes, Thomas Jolley owned two hundred acres of land, three hired servants, ten bought servants, and seventy negros." (It is probable this was Thomas Jolley of Cofton Hall, who was a known adherent of Charles the First, and probably after his execution was compelled to leave home with his son John, following Prince Rupert to the West Indies. At the Restoration he was reinstated in his estates in England. He was high sheriff of Worcester County during the reign of Charles the First, and was reinstated in that office after Charles the Second's accession to the throne.[1] His father, William Jolliffe, was high sheriff of Stafford County during the reign of Charles the First.) "Cofton Hackett came to the Jolliffe family through Edward Skinner, a rich clothier of Ledbury, who died in 1632, aged 90 years. He left six sons and six daughters. His oldest son, Richard, settled at Cofton; a younger at Ledbury (now belonging to Michael Biddulph); a third at Underdown; a fourth at Hillhouse, near Ledbury. Richard Skinner's daughter Margaret married a Jolliffe, and by her the estate passed to them." At Cofton, St. Michael's Church, are found the following,—namely, "Margaret, daughter of Sir Edward Littleton, Knt., of Pillaton Hall, Stafford, wife of Richard Skinner, who died August 25th, 1651, aged 63." On the north wall the following: "Margaret Skinner, wife of Thomas Jolliffe of Cofton, by whom she had issue five sons and two daughters. She died January 6th, 1647, aged 27 years and two months." On a marble monument fixed to the east wall of the chancel, the arms of Jolliffe with the

---

[1] "High sheriffs were attended by from fifty to one hundred retainers, in rich livery on horseback." (Evelin.)

following inscription: "Thomas Jolliffe de Leek arminger, ab antiqua profapia in agro Staffordiensi oriundus," etc. "Obiit October 23d, 1693, æt. 76." In the dining parlor is a picture of this Mr. Thomas Jolliffe (by Vandyck), with a key in his hand, which, the tradition of the family says, was given him by King Charles the First when in prison, that he might have access to him when he pleased. It is probable this was painted after the king's affairs were quite desperate, as Mr. Jolliffe is represented with a melancholy, desponding countenance, his pistols and sword hanging on a pillar before him, as if he were saying, "Hic armæstunque repono." He continued faithful to his sovereign to the last, and attended his execution. (T. R. Nash, Collections, Worcestershire.)

Down to this point the English and American ancestry are the same. In following up the history of this family in the direct line from the earliest consecutive records in England in the fourteenth century down to the present generation the recurrence of the same names transmitted from father to son has been most conspicuous, those of William, John, and Thomas occurring in every generation, thirteen in all, without break, except in one instance, where Joseph was substituted, and even then his two brothers were named John and Thomas.

5. Benjamin Jolliffe (the English heir) of Cofton Hall, in the county of Worcester, married Mary, youngest daughter of John Jolliffe, of London, a merchant (his second cousin, and a sister of Sir William Jolliffe). They had children, Thomas of Cofton Hall, who died, unmarried, in 1758; William, who died, unmarried, at Aleppo; John of Petersfield Haunts; Rebecca, who married Humphrey Lowe, of Bumsgrove, in Worcestershire; Annie, who married Robert Biddulph, of Ledbury. Mr. Jolliffe died October 28, 1719, aged seventy-four years. His wife died November 18, 1699, aged thirty-one years. Their bodies both lie in St. Michael's Church, Cofton. Thomas Jolliffe, son of Benjamin, died in 1758, and left Cofton Hall to his niece, Mrs. Lowe, for life, entailed on his nephew, Robert Biddulph, of Ledbury, Worcestershire. This will was contested on a plea of insanity, but it did not hold. His body lie in St. Michael's, Cofton. John Jolliffe, son of Benjamin, and of Petersfield Haunts, married (first) Katherine, daughter of Robert Mitchell, of Petersfield, and left no children; married (second) Mary, daughter and heiress of Samuel Holden, of London, and had issue, William Jolliffe, M.P.; Thomas Samuel Jolliffe, M.P.; Jane Jolliffe, who did not marry.

John Jolliffe died in 1771.

Benjamin Jolliffe was high sheriff of Worcester County during the reign of William and Mary, and his cousin, William Jolliffe, was the sheriff of Stafford County at the same time. "In St. Michael's Church at Cofton is to be found a monument to Benjamin Jolliffe, who died October 28th, 1719, aged 74; also one to his wife, who died November 18th, 1699, aged 31; and a very handsome one to his son Thomas Jolliffe, erected by his niece, Mrs. Lowe, to whom he left Cofton Hall for life." "The Manor of Bromsgrove belonged to the Earl of Ormond and Wiltshire, assigned to Margaret, wife of Thomas Boleyn, afterward Earl of Ormond and Wiltshire, and father of Annie Boleyn. Afterward came to Richard Fermor, and, by his attainder, to the Crown, on the 4th of December, Henry the Eighth; the King granted it to John Dudley, Viscount Lisle; he was attainted and executed, and it again went to the Crown; then it passed to the Jolliffes of Cofton Hackett." "Bunhill Manor, in the parish of Bromsgrove, belonged to the Jolliffes of Cofton Hackett." (T. R. Nash, Worcester Antiquities.)

6. John Jolliffe, third son of Benjamin, represented the borough of Petersfield in Parliament, anno 1763. His son, William Jolliffe, M.P., married Eleanor, daughter and heiress of Sir Richard Hylton of Hayton Castle, in Cumberland. Their children were Hylton Jolliffe, Rev. William Jolliffe (who married Julia Pytcher), and three daughters. Thomas Samuel Jolliffe, M.P., second son of John, of Petersfield, succeeded his father as member of Parliament for Petersfield; married, 1778, Mary-Annie, daughter and heiress of —— Twyford, Esq., of Kilmersdon, county of Somerset. He died June 6, 1824. His seat was known as Ammerdown Park. His children were John Twyford (the heir), Ammerdown Park; Thomas Robert (in holy orders); and Charles (an officer, who fell at Waterloo). "The following portraiture of a gentleman (by Savage) was intended for John Jolliffe, of Petersfield, who died 1771:

'A graceful mien, engaging in address;
Looks which at once each winning charm express;
A life where love, by wisdom polished, shines;
Where wisdom's self again by love refines;
Where we to chance for friendship never trust
Nor ever dread from sudden whim disgust;
To social manners, and the heart humane;
A nature ever great, and never vain;
A wit that no licentious coarseness knows;
The sense that unassuming candour shows;
Reason, by narrow principles unchecked,
Slave to no party, Bigot to no sect;

Knowledge of various life, of learning, too:
Thence taste, thence truth, which will from taste ensue;
Unwilling censure, though a judgment clear;
A smile indulgent, and that smile sincere;
An humble though an elevated mind;
A pride, its pleasure but to serve mankind;
If these esteem and admiration raise,
Give true delight and gain unflattering praise;
In our bright view the accomplished man we see,
These graces all are thine, and thou wert he.' "

"At Merstham Surry were living the descendants of the family of Jolliffes of very ancient standing in the counties of Worcester and Shropshire. Merstham Place was erected by William Jolliffe, who purchased the Manor in 1788. He died in 1802."

"The Church of St. Catherine's is situated on a knoll at the east end of the village. It was erected in the later English style of architecture, and contained some very handsome monuments of the Jolliffe family, and a curious font of highly polished Sussex marble, sufficiently deep for dipping an infant." (Topographical Description of England.)

"At Pleshy, Essex County, in an old church, against the south wall of the chancel, is a handsome monument to Sir William Jolliffe, Knt., who died 1749. The castle is of Roman origin, and passed to the Jolliffe family after Elizabeth's reign." (History of the Antiquities of Worcester.)

"September 20th, 1779, the wagons began loading the coals from the new won colliery on Waldridge Fell near Chester Lee Street (being the first from that colliery belonging to William Jolliffe, Esquire) to Fathfield Straith. Some thousand people attended, preceded by a band of music, colors flying, etc. In the afternoon they all returned to the houses near the colliery, where they partook of a sheep roasted whole, six sheep in quarters, and half an ox, which was washed down with eighteen barrels of good ale. The bells of Chester were rung at intervals during the day." (Border Sketches.)

For records of the Jolliffe family in England see

Berry's Essex Genealogy, page 122.
Burke's Commoners of Great Britain, vol. i. page 517.
Burke's *L*anded Gentry of Great Britain, vols. ii., iii., iv., and v.
Hutchins's Dorset, vol. iii. page 633.
Burke's Royal Families of Great Britain, vol. i. page 70.
Harlaen Society, 1-105.
Nash's Worcestershire, vol. i. page 251.
Shaw's Staffordshire.

SUMMARY OF THE HISTORY OF THE JOLLIFFE FAMILY OF ENGLAND.

1. John Jollie, of Leek, county of Stafford, was living about the middle of the fifteenth century (was probably born about 1510), "married Margaret, daughter of Ranchy." Their first son died without issue. Their second son was Thomas. (John Jolli probably had brothers Richard, of Canning Court, in the parish of Pulha, county of Dorset (who had sons John and Edmund), and Henry, who was a B.A., 1523, and dean of Bristol, 1554, etc.).

2. Thomas Jolli, of Leek, county of Stafford, and Buglawton, in Cheshire. Married (first) Margaret, daughter of Lawrence Swettenham, of Someford, county of Chester. Had a son, William Jolli, of Bothoms, in Staffordshire, born 1584, and a son, Thomas Jolli, of Leek, county of Staffordshire, lord mayor of London, 1615, whose son was Sir John Jolles, of London, alderman, born July 23, 1606, and he had a son, Sir William Jolliffe, who was knighted for building the London bridge.

3. William Jollie, of Bothoms, parish of Chedleton, in Staffordshire, born 1584, died June 11, 1669, aged eighty-five. Married Annie, daughter of Benedict Webb, of Kingwood, in county of Gloucester. They had a son, Thomas Jolli, or Jolliffe, of Cofton Hall, county of Worcester, and a son, Sir William Jolli, or Jolliffe, of Careswell Castle, county of Stafford, and a daughter Elizabeth, married Roland Hill.

4. Thomas Jollie, or Jolliffe, Esq., of Cofton Hall, county of Worcester, died October 23, 1693, aged seventy-six. One of His Majesty's justices, 1660, wedded (first) Margaret, daughter and coheir of Richard Skinner of Cofton Hall, county of Worcester (by Margaret, daughter of Sir Edward Littleton, Knight, of Pillaton, and Margaret, his wife, daughter and co-heir of Sir William Devereux, son of Walter, Viscount Hereford), by whom he had William, died aged thirteen; Thomas, died aged seventeen; John (the American heir); Benjamin (the English heir); Annie, married Alexander Felton; Margaret, married Filson Bruin. His wife Margaret died January 6, 1647, aged twenty-seven. He wedded (second) Mary, daughter of Sir Gabriel Lowe, of Newark, county of Gloucester, Knight. Had one son, William, who died unmarried in London, 1680, aged twenty-three. His wife Mary died 1663. He attended Charles I. to the place of execution.

5. Benjamin Jolliffe (the English heir) died 1719, aged seventy-four. Married Mary, youngest daughter of John Jolliffe, of London, merchant, sister of Sir William Jolliffe (and his second cousin). They had Thomas, died unmarried; William, died unmarried in Aleppo; John (his heir), of Petersfield Haunts; Rebecca Lowe, and Annie Biddulph.

6. John Jolliffe (the American) died 1716, about seventy-five years old. Married Mary Rigglesworth, daughter and heiress of Peter Rigglesworth, of Norfolk County, Colony of Virginia. They had issue Joseph, Thomas, John, Peter, Sarah (Lowe), Elizabeth (Hasgood), and Mary (Bacon).

EXTRACTS FROM OLD RECORDS OF THE JOLLIFFE FAMILY.

Pedigree of Jolliffe.

First.—Ricardus Joleiff de Canning Court in p'ochia de Pulha in
"1505 or 10" Com. Dorset. —— relict —— Rogers de Com. Som.

Second.—Johannes Joleiff de Canning Court in Com. Dorset fil.
"1535 or 40" et heres —— Elizab. filia et coh Robti
{ Will proved Jan. 30, 1583 } Newman de Fifeild Magdalen in Com. Dorset.

John Jollife of Typhed Magdalen in the County of Dorset. 29 October 1583, proved 30 January 1583. To the poor people of Stower Preaux, Stower Estower and Typhed Magdalen. To eldest daughter Rebecca Joliffe and daughter Susan Joliffe at ages of fourteen years. Son John Joliffe. Mother in law Helen Newman, widow, late wife of Robert Newman deceased. Reference to a lease granted to father Richard Joliffe, 20 December 22 Elizabeth. (1580) Father still living. To brother Edmond Joliffe. To kinswoman Christian Galler. To sister Mary Joliffe. To brother John Joliffe. Wife Elizabeth Joliffe to be sole executrix. Uncle Henry Newman, brother in law Richard Estemond, brother Edmond Jolife, Nicholas Joyce and Nicholas Clarke, Vicar of Fifeped, to be overseers. (Butts, 23.)

Third. Rebecca vxor Wili. Starre de Bradford in Com. Dorset Johannes Jolliffe de Estower in Com. Dors. fil. et. hæres.

Patris et Matris Sup'stes 1623.

Katherin da. of Johes Henninge de Paxwell in Com. Dorset Susanna vx. Will: Holman de Estower in Com. Dorset. Letters issued forth 9 December 1639, to Catherine Joliffe relict of John Joliffe lately of East Stower in the County of Dorset deceased, to administer on his goods, &c.

Admon. Act Book (1639) fo. 89.

Fourth.—Ricardus Joleiff fil et hær ætat. 12 annoru 1623. Johannes æt. 8. Rob'tus æt. 4. Georgius æt. 3. Catherine æt. 14. Dorothea æt. 13.

Signed Jo. Joyliffe.

Harl. MS. 1166, fo. 32b.

"Memorandum that George Joyliffe, Doctor in Physicke, ye Sixteenth day of November 1658 made his last will." Proved 24 November, 1658. My body to be buried with as little funeral pomp as may be. To my cousin Francis (my servant) the sum of Fifty pounds to be paid when all my debts are satisfied. To my maid servant Elizabeth five pounds and to Susan four pounds. To my cousin Francis (as above) all my Latin Books. To my daughter Katherine five hundred pounds, with the interest thereof, to be paid at the age of sixteen or the day of marriage, and the same to be put out for her use by my brother William Bigg and my cousin Richard Newman. All the residue of my estate to my loving wife Ann Joyliffe and she to be executrix. Brother William to be overseer. None of these legacies to be paid or disposed of until Mrs. Mymin's account be satisfied and paid. Wit. Thomas Ffrewan and Sara Mills. (Wootton, 631.)

Anne Joyliffe, relict and executrix of George Joyliffe, late Doctor of Phisic, 25 May 1660, proved November 1660. My body to be buried in Trinity church near Garlick Hill, London, near the body of my late husband. To my daughter Katherine Joyliffe, one thousand pounds, to be paid her at the age of sixteen years. A reference to a legacy of five hundred pounds left to her by the husband of the testatrix and to be paid her at the same age. The amount of this legacy to be recovered out of a debt due the said George by one Francis Drake of Walton, in the county of Surry. If that debt should not be recovered then five hundred pounds more to make the thousand pounds fifteen hundred. To my mother Mary Bigg one hundred and fifty pounds. To my brother John Bigg one hundred pounds. To Francis Cave, nephew to my said husband, forty pounds, to Alice Cave, his sister, ten pounds. To my said daughter Katherine my diamond ring set with one stone only, my diamond locket, my plate, linen and other household stuff. My brother William Bigg to be executor.

Wit. St. Frewen, Thomas Frewen, Miles Beales.

A codicil refers to fifteen hundred pounds secured in the names of Sir Charles Harford, my cousin Newman and my cousin Frewen, in trust for my use, and refers also to a deed from my brother Joyliffe. (Nabbs, 285.)

Thankful Frewen, of St. Andrew, Holborn, in the County of Middlesex, esq., in his will of 25 September, 1656, proved 18 March, 1656, mentions, among others, his brother Accepted Frewen, cousin George Joyliffe, Doctor in Physick, niece Ann Joyliffe, wife of the said Dr. Joyliffe and Sister Mary Bigg. (Ruthen, 110.)

John Frewen the elder, of Northiham, in the county of Sussex, clerk, aged, &c., in his will, dated 1 June 1627, mentions son Accepted Frewen (President of Magdalen College, Oxford), son Thankfull Frewen and daughter Mary, wife of John Bigg, lands, &c., in Sussex and in Newenden and Sandherst, Kent. (Barrington, 38.)

From the "Roll of the Royal College of Physicians of London, compiled from the Annals of the College and from other Authentic Sources, by William Munk, M.D., Fellow of the College, etc., etc.," previously referred to, we learn that "George Joyliffe, M.D., was born at East Stower in Dorsetshire. In the early part of 1637 he was entered a commoner of Wadham College, Oxford, where he remained about two years, and then removed to Pembroke College, as a member of which he took the two degrees in arts, A.B. 4th June, 1640; A.M. 20th April, 1643. He then entered on the study of physic, pursued anatomy with the utmost diligence, 'and with help (as Wood says) of Dr. Clayton, Master of his College, and the King's professor of physic, made some discovery of that fourth set of vessels plainly differing from veins, arteries and nerves, now called the lymphatics.' He finally removed to Clare Hall, Cambridge, and, having there proceeded doctor of medicine, settled in London; was admitted a candidate of the College of Physicians, 4th April, 1653; and a Fellow, 25th June, 1658. Dr. Joyliffe lived in Garlick Hill;

ı, as I learn from Hamey, died 11th November, 1658, being then ·ely forty years of age." He was a brother of John Joyliffe, Esq., Boston; we are told by Savage was of "Boston 1656, m/28 Jan. ;7, Ann wid. and ex'trix of Robert Knight, who had also been wid. l ex'trix of Thomas Cromwell, the wealthy privateersman, had y ch. Hannah, b. 9 May, 1690. Died November 23, 1701; he had ·n blind, and laboured under many infirmities for a long time."

GENERAL NOTES RELATING TO THE JOLLIFFE FAMILY.

"INDENTURE relating to the founding of a Free Grammar School by one Jolephi, Mr. of Arts, borne in Stratford." (Leland.) (The founder's name was really Thomas Jolyffe, as shown by the indenture.) This school was directed to be maintained by the corporation in the charter granted to the town in 7 Edw. VI. (1553). "Et dicendo, ye shall paye specially for the sowles of Maister Thom's Jolyffe, Johne and Joh'nne his faader and modur, and ye sowles of all brethers and susters of the said Gilde and all Cristin sowles, sayinge of youre Charyte a pater noster and a ave." (See Dugdale's Hist. of Stratford-upon-the-Avon.)

Upon a tablet in the wall of this school is the following: "Founded by Thomas Jolyffe—1182. Refounded by King Edward VI.—1573."

Extract from Douglass Campbell's book, "The Puritan in Holland, England, and America:" "During the reign of Edward VI. some grammar schools—we shall now call them Latin or High schools—eighteen for the whole kingdom, were established by Reformers of his government. At various times a few more were added by private individuals. One of these rare schools founded at Stratford-on-Avon, by a native of that town who had gone up to London and become Lord Mayor, bore the name of William Shakespeare on its rolls. But for the good fortune of his townsmen he might have died mute and inglorious."

"In the Miller's Tale we are told of 'Absolon' how that when at eventide he had taken up his 'Gitene,' Forth he goeth, Jolif and amorous, to the window of his lady love."

In MS. Harl., 1537, the following: "(31aa) Radulphus de Frecheville et Robertus frater ej., Will Jolyff et Will Savage dant dim, more, pro uno brevi." (Ext. Fix. de Cancell. 25 Ed. II., M 22 Derb.)

"Henry Jolliff, B.D., also dean of Bristol, fourth stall Prebendary of Worcester, 1541."

"Monsr. Will de Careswell was a tilter at the Knights' Tournament at Dunstable 7 Edw. III. Had arms D'argent frette de goules ore un fece d'asure."

"1576 John Leigh married Joan, dau. and heir of Sir John Olleph of Wickham, Kent, all of London."

"Henry Jolliff, B.A. 1523-4 and M.A. 1527, appears to have been fellow successively of Clare Hall and Michaelshouse. He served the office of Proctor of the University of Canterbury, 1537, and subsequently proceeded B.D. He became Rector of Bishops Hampton, in the county of Worcester, 1538, and was appointed one of the Canons of the Cathedral Church of Worcester by the charter of refoundation Jan. 24, 1541–2. He refused to subscribe Bishop Hoopes' Articles at his visitations of the Diocese of Worcester, 1550. He was installed Dean of Bristol Sept. 9, 1554, and attended Archbishop Cranmer's second trial at Oxford, Sept. 1555. Adhering to the Roman Catholic faith, he was on the succession of Queen Elizabeth deprived of all his preferments and went to Louvain. He died about Jan. 28, 1573–4 whilst abroad, when letters of administration of his effects were granted by prerogative Court of Canterbury to William Seres, a famous London publisher. Mr. Jolliff was author of 'Epistola Pio V., pontifici Maximo,' 1569, 'Contra Ridlæum,' &c., &c., &c." (From Athenæ Cantabrigienses.)

"Mary Hastings, wife of Wm. Jolliffe of Carveswell Castle, Co. Stafford, died 12th mo., 4th, 1678, buried in St. Martins in the Fields." (Collectanea Topographica et Genealogica.)

"Extracts from the Registers of Chute, Co. Wilts. Burials at Chute, May 19, 1645; Frauncis, wife of Henry Jolly (Vicar). The following are entries of Henry Jolly's (Vicar) children: John, bapt. May 15, 1636; Henry, bapt. Apr. 29, 1637; Mary, bapt. Aug. 7, 1638; Annie, bapt. Sep. 7, 1639; Frauncis, a son, bapt. Feb. 9, 1642 and Buried May 28, 1643; Francis, a daughter, bapt. May 12, Buried May 14, 1644.

"By his second wife, Mary Vincent: Luce, bapt. May 5, 1651; William, bapt. Jan. 10, 1652; Anna Maria, bapt. Jan. 14, 1657.

"Henry Jolly, Vicar 1634 to circa 1682."

"In the northwestern recess of St. Dunstan's Church the following: Henry Jones, Clockmaker, son of William Jones, Vicar of Bolden, Co. of Southampton, died Nov. 20, 1697, æt. 63; his wife was (widow) Hannah, dau. of Otwell Jolly of Bently, Co. Stafford." (Church Notes and Burials of St. Dunstan's in West London.)

"Claude Joly, a French writer, born in Paris 1607, Canon of Notre Dame in 1631, lived to the age of 93, died 1700. Left a fine library. Was the author of many civil and religious works."

"Guy Jolly, King's Counsellor at the chatlet, attached to the Cardinal Retz as secty. Published at Amsterdam some memoirs 1648 to 1665."

"A Mary Jolly came to Virginia in the Bark Thomas, Henry Lavender, Mr. She and her companions were examined at Gravesend touching their religions 21 Aug., 1635." (26a–712, vol. xv. page 145.)

"One Jollye of Leek County of Stafford Aug. 27, 1614."

"One Joles was Lord Mayor of London in 1615."

"On the Parochial register of Westbourne, Co. of Sussex, where many entries of Baptisms of the Jollyffe family are found. Among the burials of persons of Second Rank are Mr. Richard Jollyffe, Feb. 19, 1666."

"A Saml. Joly allowed to reside in England Dec. 4, 1681."

"Mary Jolly made a free citizen Dec. 16, 1687."

"John Jollop was witness to a will of Henry Andrews, Sen., Yeoman Lavanter, Mar. 13, 1652."

"A John Jolliffe wrote a Cumberland Guide and Directory in 1726."

"May 19, 1743, Wm. Sergeant and Ann Jolly both of St. George." (The Rolls Chapel Register.)

"John Jolliffe, of Boston, Mass., was one of the signers of a petition acknowledging the King's authority. It was presented to the Court in Oct. 1660. He was elected a Selectman March 15, 1674–5. He was appointed a trustee to receive contributions for the ransom of certain captives Sept. 1677. Was made a fire commissioner for South Quarter. Helped buy Deer Island from the Indians after being held by the English 55 years. He took a prominent part in the affairs of 1689 when the Governor was imprisoned. He was chosen Recorder March 17, 1691. His name was written in great variety. Mr. John Jolliffe, of Boston, was a gentleman of wealth and consideration from 1663 to the time of his death which occurred Nov. 23, 1701. He lived in what is now Devonshire street, between Milk and Water streets. It was one of the few streets that retained its name when the Selectmen changed them in 1708, being known as Jolliffe's Lane till 1798. John Jolliffe left a will dated Feb. 17, 1699–1700, witnessed by Anthony Checkly, Samuel Lynde, Edward Creeke and Benjamin Stone. It runs as follows: 'To friends in England, viz.: Katherine Bowles, dau. of my brother Dr. Geo. Jolliffe 20 shillings, Katherine Cooke and Alice Moxley daus. to my Sister Dorothy Cane 20 shillings each. To John Cooke of London Merchant son of my sister Martha 20 shillings. To Sister Spicer dau. of my sister Rebecca Wolcott 20 shillings. To John Drake son of my Sister Margaret Drake 20 shillings. To Margaret and Catherine Drake daus. of my Sister Margaret Drake 20 shillings each. To Esther dau. of my Sister Mary Boss sometime wife of James Boss of Shepton Mallets in County of Somerset 20 shillings. To Rev. Saml Willard of Boston £5. To Mr. Simon W. son of said

Saml £5. To the poor of the town £10. To Martha Ballard dau. of my late wife and now wife of Mr. James Ballard of Boston, house and land in Boston now in the occupation of Capt. Nathl. Byfield, sold to me by mortgage of Richard Price late of Boston Merchant decsd, for £300. All else to go to said dau. in law Martha Ballard who with husband to be exectrs.' This gentleman bore the same arms as John Jolliffe, of London, Governor of the Muscovy Company, and descended from the Jolliffes of Bothoms in Stafford County. The same arms were also borne by the family of Carverswell Castle. (Guellam's Heraldry.) (Taken from Drake's Histor. Antiq. of Boston.)

"At Upton Snodesbury, Worcester, in the fourth aisle of the Rectory. Thomas Jolley, June 28, 1704 aged 87 years 9 mos."

"Thos. Jolly of Whittington, Derbyshire, was excommunicated for not attending church."

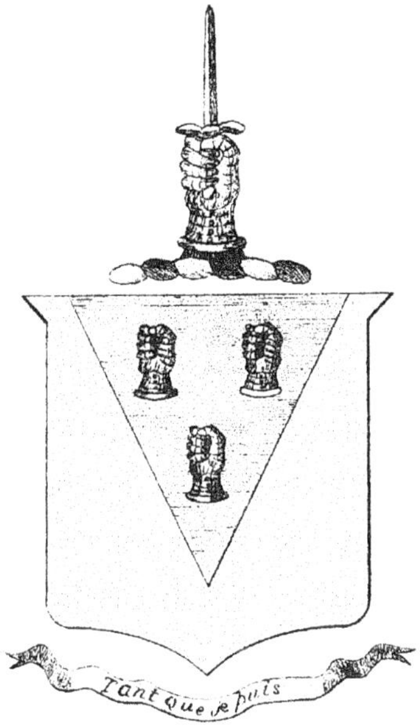

Jolliffe.

ARMS:

ARGENT ON A PILE AZURE, THREE DEXTER GAUNTLETS OF THE FIELD.

CREST:

A CUBIT ARM ERECT VESTED AND CUFFED, THE SLEEVE CHARGED WITH A PILE ARGENT, THE HAND GRASPING A SWORD PPD.

MOTTO:

"TANT QUE JE PUIS."

HISTORICAL NOTES AND PEDIGREE OF THE JOLLIFFE FAMILY OF VIRGINIA.

Family Record of John Jolliffe (the American heir of Thomas Jolliffe of Cofton Hall, England) and Mary Rigglesworth, his wife. Married about the year 1662 or 1663.

Joseph Jolliffe, born about 1663 or 1665;
John Jolliffe,
Thomas Jolliffe,
Peter Jolliffe,
Sarah (Jolliffe) Lowe; husband was Henry Lowe;
Elizabeth (Jolliffe) Hasgood; husband was Thomas Hasgood;
Mary (Jolliffe) Bacon; husband was John Bacon.

John Jolliffe (the American heir of Thomas Jolliffe of Cofton Hall and Margaret Skinner, his wife) was born in England about the year 1642 or 1643, and came to America when very young, soon after the execution of Charles I. I think he was either connected with the fleet of Prince Rupert, which was driven by Admiral Blake to the West Indies in 1651, or he may have participated with his father in the battle of Worcester, fought September 3, 1651. It was quite common for young boys of from ten to fifteen years of age to enter the army at that time.[1] He settled on the western branch of Elizabeth River, Norfolk County, Virginia, and on January 22, 1562, bought of John Lawrence, for a good consideration, one hundred acres of land.[2] He soon acquired other lands by pur-

---

[1] "(1655) Many of the recent emigrants had been royalists in England, good officers in the war, men of education, of property, and of condition. . . . Virginia had long been the home of its inhabitants. 'Among many other blessings,' said their statute-book, 'God Almighty hath vouchsafed increase of children to this Colony; who are now multiplied to a considerable number;' and the huts in the Wilderness were as full as the birds' nests of the woods. The hospitality of the Virginians became proverbial. Labor was valuable; land was cheap; competence promptly followed industry. It was 'the best poor man's country in the world.'"

[2] The first time the name of Jolliff is mentioned is in the indenture, which is as follows: "This Indenture, made this 18th day of October, in the year of our Lord God 1651, between Francis Bright of Elizabeth River, in the County of Lower Norfolk, planter, of the shore part, and John Lawrence of the County

chase and grants for bringing into the colony persons unable to pay their own way, the law giving fifty acres of land for every such person.[1] He built one of the first grist-mills ever erected in

---

of Nansemond, planter, on the other part, witnesseth, that the said Francis Bright, for and in consideration of one horsman's coat and two pair of shoes to him in hand, paid before the delivery of the same, presents, hath given, granted, and to farm let, and by those present, doth give, grant, and to farmlet, all that parcel of land containing 100 acres of land, he holdeth from Wm. Eyres of Nansemond, the said Eyres bought of Edward Selby, late of Elizabeth River, situated and lying upon a creek in Elizabeth River aforesaid, and joining upon the land of Richard Jennings, and being part of the said pattent to the said Jennings, to have and to hold, the said 100 acres of land, viz:—all the privilege appertaining thereunto, belonging, or in any way, appertaining unto the said John Lawrence, his Executors and assignes, from the date of these present, unto the end and term, and for and during the whole term of 18 years then next and immediately ensuing, and fully to be complete and ended without impeachment of any right, yielding and paying, therefor, unto the aforesaid Wm. Eyres, or his assignes, hereby, on new yearsday, or the first day of January one good fatted capon, at the new dwelling house of the said Wm. Eyres, situated in Nansemond aforesaid, provided always, and it is agreed and concluded upon, between the parties above named, that whether the said John Lawrence his executors, or assignes, or any other, by his appointment, shall molest or disturb, any cattle belonging unto the said Wm. Eyres, or his executors, or assignes, feeding, or being upon the land, or any part thereof, and in case there be any such molestation, or disturbance, unlawfully, the said John Lawrence shall pay unto the said Wm. Eyres one hogshead of tobacco for every such disturbance.

"In witness of the truth of these promices, the parties have to these present, jointly set to their hand and seals, dated the day and year first above written.

"FRANCIS (X) BRIGHT & seal
his mark
JOHN W. (X) LAWRENCE & seal.

"Signed and sealed Oct. 17, 1651.
"in the presence of
"JACOB DOOLY,
WALTER T. GRIMES.

"I, John Lawrence, do assign over this indenture, viz;—the right and title of the land therein expressed, for a good consideration, to John Jolliff, his heirs, executors, and assignes, for them, he or them, quietly to enjoy it.

"Witness my hand this 22nd day of January 1652.

his mark
"JOHN W. (X) LAWRENCE."

[1] "To All &c Whereas &c Now know yee That I ye said Richard Bennet Esq &c Give & Grant unto John Jolliffe 200 acres of Land Situate or being in ye County of Lower Norfolke, Beginning att a mark[d] beach and Soe running for

Virginia, having obtained from His Majesty's Council a permit therefor. He married, about the year 1662, Mary, only daughter and heiress of Peter Rigglesworth, of Norfolk County, Virginia, by

---

length South West by South 320 poles to a mark^{d} white oake and Soe for breath North West by West 100 poles to a mark^{d} pine and Soe againe for length North East by North 320 poles to a Mark^{d} white Oake and Soe South East by East 100 poles to ye first Mark^{d} tree, The said land being due unto ye said John Jolliffe by and for ye transportation of four persons into this Colony & To have and to hold &c Yeilding & paying & wch payment is to be made 7 years after ye first grant or sealing thereof and not before, Provided &c Dated ye 30th of May 1653.

"JON CORYE, AR LEWIS, JAMES HUNTER, MARY COOPER."

"To All &c Whereas &c Now know yee That I yee said Richard Bennet Esqr &c Give & Grant unto John Jolliffe 150 acres of *L*and, Situate or being in ye County of Isle of Wight, Beginning at a marked white Oake and Soe running for breath North 75 poles, joining to Mr. Nasworthies land to a markd Oake and Soe for length West 320 poles; butting on ye land of Mr Jones, and Soe South 75 poles; for breath butting on ye *L*and of Mr Oudlant and soe againe for length East 320 poles joining to ye land of Mr Oudlant to ye first mentioned tree, The said land being due unto ye Said John Jolliffe by and for ye transportation of three persons into this Colony &c. To have and to hold &c Yeilding & Paying & which payment &c Dated ye 30th of May 1658.

"ANNE MARSHALL, THOS KEMP, REB BENNETT."

"To All &c Whereas &c now know yee That I ye Sd Richard Bennet Esqr &c Give and Grant unto John Jolliffe two hundred and fifty acres of *L*and lying in ye County of Nansemond on ye Westward side of ye Westward branch of Nansemond river, and beginning at a marked red Oake, and running for length South West by West 320 poles to a Small red Oake markd on ye land of James Arthur & Peter Ellis & soe South East by South 125 poles to a marked red oake & soe North East by East 320 poles unto a Markd red oak standing by ye branch side, Soe running up by or nigh ye maine branch side to ye first mentioned markd tree, The said land being formerly granted unto John *L*andman by patent dated ye 9th of April 1648 & purchased of ye sd *L*andman by ye Said John Jolliffe To have and to hold &c Yeilding & paying & which payment is to be made 7 years after ye first grant or Sealing thereof, and not before Provided &c Dated ye 4th of July 1658."

"To all &c whereas &c now Know Ye that I the said Francis Moryson Esq Governor &c give and grant unto John Jolliffe 200 acres of *L*and Situate or being in the County of *L*ower Norfolk. Beginning at a marked Beach and so running for *L*ength South West by South 320 poles to a marked white Oak and so for breadth North West by West 100 poles to a marked Pine and so again for *L*ength North East by North 320 poles to a marked white Oak & so South-East by East 100 poles to the first mentioned tree the said *L*and being formerly granted unto John Jolliffe by Patent dated the 30 of May 1653 and now renewed

whom he had four sons and three daughters,—viz., Joseph, John, Thomas, Peter, Sarah, Elizabeth, and Mary. They deeded each of their children one hundred acres of land during their life or when they attained age or were married. By his wife Mary, John Jolliffe acquired considerable property, which was disposed of to his children during his lifetime or willed to them at his death. His wife died about the year 1704–5, and he died the year 1716, his will bearing date November 28, 1716. When Governor Spottswood came over as governor of the colony he undertook to rectify the great abuses found to exist in the Land Office. To this end he required all parties who had been granted lands by the process of "seating and planting" to come forward and re-enter their lands. John Jolliffe's son Thomas thus re-entered eight hundred and sixty-seven acres of land August 12, 1713, owned by the family, and in a series of deeds made them over to his brothers and sisters just as they had formerly been bestowed by John and Mary, his wife; these deeds bear date November 18, 1714. By his will John Jolliffe left his farm on which he resided to his son Joseph. It contained two hundred and sixty-seven acres. His mill was left to John Bacon and his wife, Mary (Jolliffe) Bacon. To his son Peter he left his "back swoard," and to each of his sons he left a gun. Joseph Jolliffe, his eldest son, was named as his executor. John Jolliffe seems to have been an educated man, possessed of some wealth when he came into the colony, which he added to during

---

in his Majesties name &c To have and to hold &c to be held &c Yeilding and paying &c provided &c dated the 13th of January 1661."

"To All &c Whereas &c Now Know Yee that I the said Sr Henry Chichely Knt., Deputy Governor &c Give and grant unto John Jolliffe 867 acres of land being at ye head of the broad Creeke of ye Westerne branch of Elizabeth river, In ye County of Lower Norfolke. Beginning at a red Oake by a branch side and running South by his old markd trees 228 poles to ye land of Thomas Cattle; Thence on his line of markt trees North West 136 poles to Thomas Cattles Corner white Oake Thence on his line South East 36 poles, Thence West 640 poles leading into a pocosson, then againe from ye first mentioned red oake West South West along ye branch side 56 poles, then West NoWest 10 poles over ye forke of ye branch to a beech, the corner tree of his old patent, thence North West by West 100 poles along ye branch to a white Oake another corner tree of his old patent, then South West by South by Markt trees 150 poles to ye land of James Murray, Then bounding on Murraye's Markt trees North West by West 260 poles to a white Oake in Murrayes line, Then South West by Markt trees 460 poles into ye first Mentioned pocoson unto ye end of the first Mentioned West line, 267 acres of wch land was formerly granted the Said Jolliffe by patent dated the 18th of Octb 1664 and 200 acres more granted Jno

his lifetime.[1] At his death he was about seventy-six years old. He seems to have always resided in Virginia, on the western branch of Elizabeth River, Norfolk County. (I think his son Joseph was named after Joseph Lowe, a brother of Sir Gabriel Lowe, his father's second wife's father, who fled to Virginia for safety after Charles I.'s execution, probably accompanying John Jolliffe.)

Jolliffe Senr. by patent dated ye 13th of January 1661, and 400 acres being due by & for ye transportation of eight persons into this Collony &c To have & to hold &c to be held &c yielding & paying &c, dated ye 20th of April 1682.

"JNO MAY.	THOS NUTT.	HERBERT SPRING.
JAMES COPPIN.	ANDREW STREET.	RICHD HEATH."
THOS DULANA.	JAMES ANST.	

[1] "The earliest mode of acquiring land in the Colony was in Virtue of five years' service to the London Co.; at the expiration of which the Adventurer was 'set free' and entitled to a 'divident' of 100 acres, which if planted and seated by the building of a house upon it within three years, entitled the planter to an additional 100 acres, if not, it reverted to the Crown. Later, each one coming to the Colony, or transporting thither, or paying the passage of others, was entitled for himself, each member of his family, or other person thus transported, to 50 acres of land, which was called a 'head right' and was transferable. Still later lands were granted upon the condition of paying an annual 'quit rent' of one shilling for every 50 acres and of planting and seating within three years." (Brock's Notes on the Spottswood Papers.)

Family Record of Joseph Jolliffe and Ruth ——, his wife. Married about the year 1694-95.

William Jolliffe, born about 1695,
and other children of whom no record;
Joseph Jolliffe married Elizabeth —— (second wife) about the year 1732, and left no children.

Joseph Jolliffe, the eldest child of John and Mary (Rigglesworth) Jolliffe, was born at his father's house, on Western Branch of Elizabeth River, Norfolk County, Virginia, about the year 1663-65. He was well educated, and I am inclined to think was a lawyer or held some office about the county clerk's office. At all events he seems to have been chosen by his brothers and sisters to administer on their estates or act as executor. He was given by his father one hundred acres of land early in life, on which he resided for some time. "Oct. 15th, 1721, Joseph Jolliffe of Norfolk Co. and Ruth his wife, deeds to John Bacon, (his brother-in-law) for consideration, their grist mill willed them by their father John Jolliffe, the mill heretofore described.

"JOSEPH JOLLIFF
RUTH JOLLIFF."

"Feb. 16, 1724, Peter Jolliff and wife Ann, and Joseph Jolliff and wife Ruth, deed to Thomas Jolliff 8½ acres land on south side of Mill Creek at head of Western Branch of Elizabeth River, for 350 pounds of tobacco.

"PETER JOLLIFF
ANN JOLLIFF
JOSEPH JOLLIFF
RUTH JOLLIFF."

He married about the year 1694 95 Ruth ——, who was living as late as 1725; he married (second) Elizabeth —— about the year 1732, and it is quite probable she survived him. "May 21, 1731, Joseph Jolliff deeds a tract of land to Aaron Bolton.

"JOSEPH JOLLIFF
RUTH JOLLIFF."

"Feb. 16, 1735, Joseph Jolliff deeds to Ann Bolton 50 acres swamp land granted Thos. Jolliff Aug. 12, 1713, (regrant) bounded by the lands of Richard Jolliff, Thos Ivy and Ann Bolton.

"JOSEPH JOLLIFF
ELIZABETH JOLLIFF."

"April 13, 1737, Joseph Jolliff of the Western Branch, in Norfolk County, deeds to Richard Bacon one whole tract of land whereon the said Jolliff now lives, and the house, lying on the Western Branch of Elizabeth River of Norfolk Co. Land left to the said Joseph Jolliff by his father John Jolliff Nov. 28, 1716, and being a patent bearing date Oct. 18, 1664. Containing 267 acres.

"JOSEPH JOLLIFF
ELIZABETH JOLLIFF."

This was the home place sold out. Where Joseph went from here cannot be determined. It would appear he was at this time an old man; his children having left him, he married a second wife late in life. The court records of Norfolk County are partially missing between 1719 and 1730, and very unfortunately the records of Nansemond County were all burned in the year 1867, after having survived three wars. These records would have given a much more complete record of Joseph Jolliff and his family, I am sure, for he seems to have drifted westward. The records speak of his children, hence there must have been others besides his son William, of whom I can find no record. (The present Mr. Josiah Jolliffe living in Norfolk County says his father has told him there was a family tradition of a William Jolliffe, brother of James Jolliffe, who had left the country, and had never been heard from since. These were no doubt the sons of Joseph and Ruth Jolliff.)

The materials are so meagre that it is almost impossible to prepare sketches of the sons and grandsons of John Jolliffe, the American ancestor of the family. Dr. William P. Palmer, who was appointed under authority from the Legislature of Virginia to make a calendar of the Virginia state papers, in noting the terrible losses to the State of valuable papers and manuscripts, says, "Losses which occurred when Jamestown became the scene of violence and conflagration. The accidents to which the colonial archives were exposed when the ancient capital on the James was deserted for the more attractive and rising city of the middle plantations, and finally when, in 1779, the latter ceased to be the seat of government; and when, upon the apprehended advance of the British forces during the Revolution, they were again removed to Richmond for safety.

It is probable many valuable manuscripts were lost by the destruction of the buildings at William and Mary College by fire, which had been left in them when the Royal Governors ceased to hold sessions of the Council within her walls. Again, in Arnold's invasion of 1781 the Richmond authorities became alarmed, and the contents of the public offices were hastily tumbled into wagons and carried off to the most unfrequented parts of the upper James and to the hills of Cumberland and Bedford, and in this transit more loss was sustained; when again the liberal and too often careless policy of the State exposed the documents in the Capitol to inquisitive followers of the Federal forces upon the occupation of Richmond in 1865, and also to the depredations of relic hunters since, as the empty envelopes endorsed as containing original letters of Washington, Jefferson, and Madison testify. But by far the most serious loss sustained was at the accidental burning of the State Court-house in Richmond in 1865, in which were consumed almost the entire records of the old General Court, from the year 1619, or thereabouts, together with records of many of the county courts carried to Richmond for safe-keeping during the civil war of 1861, with also the records of the Court of Appeals. The importance of this disaster can only be realized when it is remembered what an important relation the General Court bore to the history of the Colony from the time when the semi-military government, which for the first year of its existence controlled its affairs, had passed away down to a comparatively late period. This august and aristocratic body was always composed of the class known at that time as 'gentlemen,' men of wealth, family, and influence. They with the Governor formed the Executive Council, who dispensed the entire patronage of the Colony, at the same time that each individual member was himself commissioned 'Colonel' by Royal authority. To this fact may probably be traced the habit in Virginia of decorating prominent men with empty military titles even to this day."

To all these and other losses cited by Dr. Palmer I would add above all the absence of those valuable historical societies which all over New England and the Middle States are as beacon-lights to the genealogist, saving him so much time and travel and throwing up for him a royal road compared to that over which the Virginia seeker has to travel. Fortunately for me, the Norfolk County records, which cover the life history of the first immigrant John Jolliffe, are nearly complete and in good order. From them I have gleaned that he was a man of education and influence, and must have come to the colony possessed of considerable means, or else as so young a man he could never have acquired so early such a large amount of property, at a time when the acquisition of property was rendered exceedingly difficult by the laws of the colony. His record shows that he identified himself largely in the material development of the country by obtaining royal permits for the establishment of industries, etc. The subsequent records of his sons and grandsons I have found much more meagre, owing to the destruction especially of the Nansemond County records, which went back to 1632, at the burning of the court-house at Suffolk in 1867, as before mentioned. So I can write very little regarding them until his grandson William appears in the early formation of the county of Frederick, and founding the town of Winchester. Here he enrolls his name among the first ten lawyers to practise in that court, then just forming, and after this the record is comparatively plain sailing.

Of the other sons of John and Mary (Rigglesworth) Jolliffe I give the following brief history: John Jolliffe, second son of John Jolliffe, of Norfolk County, married Martha ——, and had issue John, Richard, Peter, Elizabeth-Bowers, Mary Taylor, Sarah-Hodges, Susanna-Bowers, Rachael, and Ann. This family lived in Norfolk County, and some of the descendants are still holding the old homesteads. John's will bears date April 5, 1736. (Jolliffe Chapel in the county of Norfolk was so called after the Rev. Josiah Jolliffe, a great-grandson of this John.) His wife Martha died in 1761 at an advanced age. Her will is dated May 9, 1761.

Thomas Jolliffe, third son of John, of Norfolk County, married (first) Elizabeth ——, who died about the year 1697. He married (second) Mary ——, who died about the year 1715. He died in the year 1731, his will bearing date September 18, 1731. He was at one time a resident of Princess Anne County, and owned a large estate near Lynnhaven Bay. He seems to have been a man of means. In his will he does not mention his children (from this I presume he had none, or else all were dead before him), but names his brother Joseph his executor.

Peter Jolliffe, fourth son of John Jolliffe, of Norfolk County, married Ann ——. They lived in Princess Anne County. September 10, 1738, they sold their old homestead in Norfolk County to John Hobgood. Their children seem to have gone into North Carolina, and his descendants are found in some of the Southern States at this time.

In order to give a better understanding of the times in which a great portion of the Jolliffes of Virginia lived, and the influences they were subjected to, I give herewith a brief sketch of the settlement of Virginia, in which many of the family were intimately connected.

A BRIEF HISTORY OF THE SETTLEMENT OF VIRGINIA.

The settlement of Virginia, briefly stated, is as follows: A number of enterprising and adventurous persons of London and Plymouth, England, petitioned the king, James I., to grant them charters for two companies "to possess and cultivate lands in America," which was granted, letters patent bearing date April 10, 1606, and the names of the corporations being "The London Company" and "The Plymouth Company." The London Company sent Captain Christopher Newport to Virginia December 20, 1606, with a colony of one hundred and five persons to commence a settlement on the island of Roanoke, now in North Carolina. By stress of weather, however, they were driven north of their destination, and entered Chesapeake Bay. Here, up a river which they called James River, on a beautiful peninsula, they founded the little colony of Jamestown in May, 1607. In the year 1619 the first legislative council was convened at Jamestown, then called James City, by Sir George Yeardley, then governor of the colony. On July 24, 1621, Sir Francis Wyatt received a commission as governor, and with it a "set of instructions" as follows: "To keep up religion of the Church of England; to be obedient to the king; not injure the natives; forget old quarrels. To be industrious, suppress drunkeness, gaming and excess in cloaths; to permit none but the Counsel and heads of hundreds to wear gold in their cloaths; none to wear silk till they made it. Not to offend foreign persons; punish piracies, and teach children, to convert the heathen. To make a catalogue of the people and their condition, of deaths, marriages and christenings; to take care of estates, keep list of all cattle. Not to plant above 100 pounds of tobacco per head; to sow great quantities of corn; to keep cows, swine, poultry, etc.; to plant mulberry trees, and make silk and take care of the Frenchmen in that work; to plant an abundance of vines. To put 'prentices to trades, and not let them forsake their trades for planting tobacco or any such useless commodity. To take care of the Dutch sent to build mills; to build water mills and block houses in every plantation. That all contracts be performed and breaches thereof punished; tenants not to be enticed away. To make salt, pitch, tar, soap, oil of walnuts, search for minerals, gems, etc., and send small quantities home. To make small quantities of tobacco, and that very good, and to keep the store houses clean."

In the year 1611 the entire population of the colony amounted to seven hundred souls, and in that year were brought to America the first cows, goats, and hogs, and twenty women, being the first white females who ever trod the soil. In 1614 tobacco was introduced from the West Indies. Among some of the first laws passed were the following: "That there shall be in every plantation, where the people used to meet for the worship of God, a house or roome sequestered for that purpose, and not to be for any temporal use whatsoever, and a place empaled in, on it, 'for the burial of the dead;' that whosoever shall absent himself from Divine service any Sunday, without an allowable excuse, shall forfeit a pound of tobacco; that the Governor shall not withdraw the inhabitants from their private labors to any service of his own, upon any colour whatsoever, and in case the public service requires employment of many hands before holding a general assembly, to give order for the same; that all trade for corn with the salvages, as well as public and private, after June next, shall be prohibited; that the proclamation for swearing and drunkeness set out by the Governor and Counsel are confirmed by this Assembly; that every dwelling house shall be pallizaded in, for defense against the Indians; that no man go or send partie without a sufficient partie well armed; that there be dew watch kept by night; that such persons of quality as shall be found delinquent in their duties being not fit to undergo corporal punishment, may notwithstanding be ymprisoned at the discretion of the commander, and for greater offenses to be subjected to a fine inflicted by the monthly court, so that it exceed not the value aforesaid."

In the year 1620 negro slaves were introduced from a Dutch ship. In 1645 coined money was introduced by act of the General Assembly, all currency up to this date being tobacco, which was the standard of value. In 1659 the notorious act for the suppression of Quakers was passed. In 1675 and 1676 Bacon rebelled against Sir William Berkley, and Jamestown was burned. March, 1692–93, an act was passed for the establishment of a post-office in the country, and the same year an act for ascertaining a place for erecting the college of William and Mary, the first college on the continent. "On August 1st, 1716, the knightly governor, Col. Alexander Spottswood, in company with a troop of horsemen consisting of 50 persons in all, with a goodly supply of provisions, ammunition and a varied assortment of liquors, set out to cross the high mountains of Virginia. After several fights with hostile savages, who dogged the footsteps of the party, at the expiration of thirty-six days, at about 1 o'clock, September 5th, 1716, Governor Spottswood, who was slightly in the advance, reached the brow of a declivity at the top of the Blue Ridge, at Swift Run Gap, and the whole glorious view burst upon his enraptured sight. For some moments, as the members of the governor's party gathered around him, not a word or sound broke the silence of the awe-inspiring scene, but they soon dismounted from their horses, and drank the health of the king. As far as the eye could reach, the most enchanting landscape presented itself. To the front of them, to the right and left, rolled miles of tall grass; the silvery streams in serpentine coils wound in and out for miles away, whilst in the distance mountain upon mountain seemed piled one upon the other, until lost in the blue and gold of the clouds, challenging the eye to define where clouds began and mountains ceased. Upon the return of Spottswood and his party, the governor, in commemoration of the event, had a number of golden horse-shoes struck, each of which had inscribed upon it, 'Sic Jurat Transcendere Montes:' 'Though he swears to cross the mountains.'" No attempt seems to have been made to make a settlement in the Shenandoah Valley until the year 1725. In 1720 the General Assembly passed an act for the creation of the counties of Spottsylvania and Brunswick, the preamble of which, and that portion relating to Spottsylvania, are here given:

"PREAMBLE: That the frontiers, towards the high mountains, are exposed to danger from the Indians, and the late settlements of the French to the westward of said mountains,

"*Enacted*, Spottsylvania county bounds upon Snow Creek up to the Mill, thence by southwest line to the River North Anna, thence by the said River as far as convenient, and thence by a line to be run over the high mountains to the River on the northwest side thereof, so as to include the northern passage through said mountains; thence down the said River till it comes against the head of Rappahannock; thence by a line to the head of Rappahannock and down that River to the mouth of Snow Creek; which tract of land, from the first of May, 1721, shall become a county, by the name of Spottsylvania county."

In 1734 another division occurred. Spottsylvania was divided and its northern half created into the county of Orange. Four years later than the above date, 1734, the county of Frederick was created by an act passed in November, 1738, which act reads as follows:

"WHEREAS: Great numbers of people have settled themselves of late upon the Rivers of Sherrando, Conhongoruton (Potomac) and Opeckon, and the branches thereof, on the northwest side of the Blue Ridge of mountains, whereby the strength of this colony and its security upon the frontiers, and His Majesty's revenue of quit-rents are likely to be much increased and augmented; for giving encouragement to such as shall see fit to settle there;

"*Be it enacted*, That all that territory and tract of land at present deemed to be a part of the County of Orange, lying on the north-west side of the top of said mountains, extending from thence northerly, westwardly and southerly beyond the said mountains to the utmost limits of Virginia, be separated from the rest of said county, and created into two distinct counties and parishes; to be divided by a line to be run from the head spring of Hedgeman River to the head spring of the River Potowmack; and that all that part of the said territory lying to the northeast of the said line, beyond the top of the said Blue Ridge, shall be one distinct county and parish, to be called by the name of the County of Frederick and Parish of Frederick; and that the rest of the said territory lying on the other side of the said line, beyond the top of the said Blue Ridge, shall be one distinct county and parish, to be called by the name of the County of Augusta, and Parish of Augusta."

Singular to relate, after Spottswood's expedition, the first settlements in the Shenandoah Valley were not made from East Virginia, but instead, the fame of the great Virginia valley for its splendid land, fine watercourses, and beautiful mountains, attracted the attention of some thrifty Germans who had settled in Pennsylvania, in York and Lancaster Counties. A number of these, led by Yost Hite, moved through Maryland and crossed the river a few miles above where now is Harper's Ferry, settling along the Potomac, with the junction of that stream with the Shenandoah westward for ten or fifteen miles. They founded a village in their midst about 1727, which they called New Mecklenburg. This was afterwards changed to Shepardstown by one Mr. Thomas Shepard, who acquired property there. These persons were simple squatters upon the land. About 1730, Richard ap Morgan, a Welshman, obtained from Governor Gooch a grant for a large body of lands which he located in the neighborhood of Shephardstown, building there a log house, supposed to be the first dwelling ever erected in the Shenandoah Valley. He was followed very shortly by Rev. Morgan Morgan, a native of Wales, who emigrated from Pennsylvania, and settled in what is now known as the county of Berkley. He was a man of exemplary piety and devoted to the church, and was instrumental in erecting the first Episcopal church in the valley of Virginia. From the settlements in Chester County, Pennsylvania, there arrived a large influx of emigrants to the new colony, among whom were many of the same faith as Penn, thrifty, well-to-do people; also a large number of Protestant Germans, all of whom settled upon the rich lands of the Shenandoah and Opecquon Creeks.[1] Among the first to obtain a grant from Governor Gooch, of Virginia, was Alexander Ross, a Quaker, who secured seventy thousand acres, locating the same north, west, and south of where now stands Winchester. This was in 1730 or thereabouts, and the ground was surveyed by Robert Brooks, 1731 and 1732. In addition to the Germans and Quakers who first came, there also came many Irish and Scotch-Irish from Lancaster County, in Pennsylvania, who settled along Back Creek and Opecquon. The route taken by these early settlers to reach the valley was from the neighborhood of York, in Pennsylvania, down through Maryland, striking the Potomac at the old Pack-Horse Ford, a mile east of Shephardstown, which at that date was simply a portion of the Indian trail, but which was the great northern and southern highway of the Indians for, possibly, centuries, along which hostile tribes had marched and camped, the Delawares going southward, the Catawbas and Shawnees going northward, frequent warlike excursions being made into this country. Much the greater part of the country between what is called the Little North Mountain and the Shenandoah River, at the first settling of the valley, was one vast prairie, covered with luxurious grass and wild strawberry vines, and even the sides of the mountains were covered with wild pea vines, which afforded the finest possible pasturage for wild animals, such as buffalo, elk,

---

[1] "Several respectable individuals of the Quaker Society thought it unjust to take possession of this valley without making the Indians some compensation for their right. Measures were adopted to effect this great object. But upon inquiry no particular tribe could be found who pretended to have any prior claim to the soil. It was considered the common hunting ground of various tribes, and not claimed by any particular nation who had authority to sell. This information was communicated to the author by two aged and highly respectable men of the Friends' Society, Isaac Brown and Lewis Neill, each of them upwards of eighty years of age, and both residents of the County of Frederick. In confirmation of this statement, a letter was written by Thomas Chaulkly to the Monthly Meeting on Opecquon on the 21st 5th Mo., 1738. . . . This excellent letter from this good man proves that the Quakers were among our earliest settlers, and that this class of people were early disposed to do justice to the natives of the country." (Kercheval.)

deer, etc., at that time very plentiful. Only along the streams and watercourses was good timber to be found, hence the early settlers chose their homes close to the borders of the streams, that they might secure wood and water in conjunction with their prairie lands.[1] At this time the Indians roamed at will over these prairies,

[1] "At this period timber was so scarce that the settlers were compelled to cut small saplings to inclose their fields. The prairie produced grass five or six feet high; and even our mountains and hills were covered with a rich growth. . . . From this state of the country, many of our first settlers turned their attention to raising large herds of horses, cattle, hogs, etc. Many of them became expert, hardy and adventurous hunters, and depended chiefly for support and money-making on the sale of skins and furs. The first houses erected by the primitive settlers were log cabins, with covers of split clapboards, and weight poles to keep them in place. They were frequently seen with earthen floors; or if wooden floors were used, they were made of split puncheons a little smoothed with the broad-axe. There were, however, a few framed and stone buildings erected previous to the war of the revolution. When improvement began, the most general mode of building was with hewn logs, a shingle roof and plank floor, the plank cut out with the whip-saw. The dress of the early settlers was of the plainest materials, generally of their own manufacture; the men's coats were generally made with broad backs, and straight short skirts, with pockets on the outside having large flaps. The waistcoats had skirts nearly half-way down to the knees and very broad pocket-flaps. The breeches were so short as barely to reach the knee, with a band surrounding the knee fastened with either brass or silver buckles. The stocking was drawn up under the knee-band and tied with a red or blue garter below the knee so as to be seen. The shoes were of coarse leather, with straps fastened with either brass or silver buckles. The hat was either of wool or fur, with a round crown not exceeding three or four inches high, with a broad brim. The neck encased in a white linen stock fastened at the back with a buckle. The female dress was generally a short gown and petticoat, made of the plainest materials; they were often seen with bare feet and arms. They usually labored with the men in the fields during the busy seasons. Furniture was of the simplest kind, that for the table consisted of a few pewter dishes, plates, and spoons, but mostly of wooden bowls, trenchers, and noggins, or of gourds and squashes. In the whole display of furniture china and silver were unknown. The hunting-shirt was universally worn by a large part of the settlers; this was a kind of loose frock, with large sleeves, open before, and so wide as to lap over a foot or more when belted. The cape was large and fringed with a ravelled piece of cloth of a different color from the shirt itself. They were generally made of linsey, coarse linen, or dressed deer-skins. The acquisition of such articles as salt, iron, and castings presented great difficulties to the first settlers. They had no stores of any kind, no salt, iron, or iron-works, nor had they money to make purchases. Peltry and furs were their only resources, or the sale of cattle and horses taken to trade for these needed articles in Frederick, Baltimore, or Philadelphia. These goods were carried by pack-horses in caravans. The usual price for a bushel of salt

and at one or two points in the valley had considerable towns: the Tuscarrorers, on Tuscarrorer Creek, near where Martinsburg now stands; the Shawnees, at the Shawnee Springs, where Winchester stands. These Indians looked upon the people from Virginia with abhorrence, whom they designated "Long Knife." and were warmly opposed to their settling in the valley. Tradition relates that the Indians did not object to the Pennsylvanians settling in the country, but from the high character of William Penn the poor simple natives believed that all of Pennsylvania's men were honest, virtuous, humane, and benevolent, but they soon found to their cost that Pennsylvanians were not much better than the others. A noted exception must be made in the case of the Quakers, who endeavored to purchase their lands from the Indians as well as from the Crown. See the beautiful letter of Thomas Chalkley, dated May 21, 1738, on this subject. In all the long and bloody border wars not a single Quaker was ever murdered or molested by an Indian, a beautiful tribute to the peace-loving principles and practices of William Penn.

For several years after the creation of Frederick County there was not sufficient population in all the territory west of Blue Ridge to justify the appointment of county officers and the organization of a county government, but October 2, 1743, "His Excellency Wm. Gooch, Esquire, Lieutenant and Commander-in-Chief of the forces of the colony and province of Virginia, by the grace of His Most Christian Majesty, Our Sovereign Lord George the Second, King, Defender of the Faith, etc.," issued commissions, as justices of the peace, to "Our Trusted and Well Beloved Morgan Morgan, Benjamin Borden, Thomas Chester, David Vance, Andrew Campbell, Marquis Calmes, Thomas Rutherford, Lewis Neill, William McMachen, Meredith Helms, George Hoge, John White and Thomas Little, gentlemen, accompanied by a dedimus for the administering of the oath of office to the appointees. On November 11, 1743, the gentlemen, having been notified of their appointment, met for the purpose of organizing a court." This meeting took place in the house of James Wood, in what is now the central portion of Winchester. Having met, Morgan Morgan and David Vance administered the oath to the others named in the commission, who, having taken their seats as justices for Frederick County, appointed James Wood clerk of the court, and Thomas Rutherford high sheriff; George Home was appointed surveyor. At this court appeared

---

was a cow and calf, the salt measured by hand in the half-bushel as lightly as possible. Tea, coffee, and sugar were unknown commodities. Every man was a soldier. The frontiers presented a succession of military camps or forts."

James Porteus, John Steerman, George Johnson, and John Newport, who were booked as attorneys. The sheriff was ordered to build a twelve-foot log house, logged above and below to secure prisoners. The next court was held December 9, when James Porteus was empowered to act as king's attorney until the pleasure of the governor could be known. Thomas Chester was appointed coroner, and took the oath of office. At this court Patrick Riley petitioned for a license "to keep an ordinary." Several others obtained licenses for ordinaries at the same time, among whom were Thomas Hart and Lewis Neill. On Friday, June 13, the ensuing month, at a meeting of the court, five more lawyers placed themselves on the roll of attorneys for Frederick County, they being William Russell, John Quinn, Gabriel Jones, WILLIAM JOLLIFFE, and Michael Ryan. At a court held February 11, 1743–44, Gabriel Jones was recommended by the justices to the governor as a suitable person for the king's attorney. May 11, 1744, the first grand jury was impanelled in the county. The first deed placed upon the records of the county was one from Abraham Pennington to Christopher Beeler for five hundred acres of land. November 13, 1751, George Ross transferred about ten acres of land to Isaac Hollingsworth, Evan Thomas, Jr., and Evan Rogers for building a Quaker meeting-house. As heretofore stated, Thomas Rutherford was the first sheriff of the county; his bondsmen, in the sum of one thousand pounds, were Meredith Helms, John Hardin, Thomas Ashby, Sr., James Seeburn, Robert Ashby, Thomas Ashby, Jr., Peter Wolff, and Robert Worthington. The second sheriff was Thomas Chester, 1745; third, Andrew Campbell, 1747; fourth, Jacob Hite, 1749; fifth, Lewis Neill, 1751; sixth, Meredith Helms, 1753. "On November 17, 1749, the Right Honorable Thomas Lord Fairfax, Baron of Cameron, in that part of Great Britain called Scotland, and proprietor of the Northern Neck, produced a special commission to be one of His Majesty's Justices of the Peace for the County, from under the hand of the Honorable Thomas Lee, Esquire, President and Commander-in-Chief of the Colony and Dominion of Virginia, and the seal of this Colony, took the oaths appointed by Act of Parliament to be taken instead of the oaths of Allegiance and Supremacy, and the oaths of abjuration, and having subscribed the teste was sworn a Justice of the Peace, and of the County Court in Chancery; Lord Fairfax producing a commission, was sworn County Lieutenant."

The following documents, copied from the first deed book and bearing date March 9, 1749, give the first glimpse of what is now Winchester, then called Fredericktown:

"Know All Men By These Presents, That I James Wood, of Frederick County, am held and firmly bound unto Morgan Morgan, Thomas Chester, David Vance, Andrew Campbell, Marquis Calmes, Thomas Rutherford, Lewis Neill, William McMachen, Meredith Helms. George Hoge, John White and Thomas Little, Gents, Justices of the said County, and their successors, in the sum of one thousand pounds, current money of Virginia, to be paid to the said Morgan Morgan, etc., and which payment well and truly to be made I bind myself, my heirs, executors and administrators firmly by these presents, and sealed with my seal, and dated this 9th day of March, 1743; The Condition of the above obligation is such that, whereas, the above-bound James Wood having laid off from the tract of land at which he now dwells, at Opeckon, in the County aforesaid, twenty-six lots of land, containing one half-acre each together with two streets running through the said lots, each of the breadth of 33 feet, as will more plainly appear by a plan thereof in the possession of the said Morgan Morgan, etc. And, whereas, the said James Wood, for divers good causes and considerations him thereunto moving, but more especially for and in consideration of the sum of Five shillings, current money, to him in hand paid, the receipt whereof he doth hereby acknowledge, hath bargained and sold, on the conditions hereinafter mentioned, all his right, title, interest, property and claim to 22 of the said lots to the aforesaid Morgan Morgan, etc., His Majesty's Justices of the said County for the time being, and their successors, to be disposed of by them for the use of the said County as they shall judge most proper," etc. "Signed, J. Wood. Sealed, and delivered in the presence of William Jolliffe, John Newport and Thomas Postgate." Wood, it appears from the above documents, did not at that time own the land, but acquired title to it upon the arrival of Lord Fairfax. In the year 1752, James Wood petitioned the General Assembly to lawfully establish his town and name it Winchester, after Winchester in England.

For twelve years after the settlement of the great valley the inhabitants enjoyed profound peace and prosperity, mingling freely with the Indians, who were passing to and fro at all times through this country. In the year 1753 emissaries from the western Indians came among the valley Indians, inviting them to cross the Alleghany Mountains, and in the spring of the year 1753 Major George Washington was sent with a letter to the French commander on the western borders, remonstrating against his encroaching upon the territory of Virginia. Soon after this the war, commonly called

"Braddock's War," began, and in 1754 Virginia raised an armed force, the command of which was given to Colonel Fry, and George Washington appointed lieutenant-colonel. In 1755 Braddock, at the head of two English regiments, was sent to reduce Fort Pitt, which resulted in a disastrous defeat. Immediately after the defeat of Braddock, Washington retreated to Winchester, in the county of Frederick, and in the autumn of 1755 began to build Fort Loudon. Here Washington resided with his army for the next two years, during which time the settlers on the frontiers were daily harassed and worried by incursions from the Indians and French. Many valuable lives were lost and property destroyed, and the people subjected to untold hardships. After the close of hostilities the valley again enjoyed a period of repose until about the year 1772, when "Dunmore's War" broke out, and raged with unabated fury all along the frontier. Before its close hostilities began with Great Britain, and for eight years the valley was kept in a state of turmoil, the inhabitants greatly harassed and excited, property depreciated and destroyed, young men drawn into the army, and the old men and women subjected to all the horrors of war and famine, added to which were the terrors of Indian scalping-parties making repeated raids throughout the whole valley section.

The Presbyterian meeting-house at Tuscarrorer, county of Berkley, was the first place where the gospel was preached publicly and divine service performed west of the Blue Ridge. About the year 1733 the Friends held religious services at private houses in the valley. The first Friends' meeting-house was a small log house erected in 1734–35, about thirty yards from the present sexton's house at Hopewell, near Ross's Spring, now known as Washington's Spring. In 1735 William Hoge,[1] having settled on land about

[1] William Hoge, a native of Musselburgh, Scotland, came to America after 1682. In the same ship was a Mr. Hume and his wife and daughter, from Paisley, Scotland. The father and mother both died at sea on their way over. William Hoge took charge of their orphan daughter and turned her over to her relatives in New York City. He settled at Perth Amboy, New Jersey. In the course of time he married this orphan, Barbara Hume, and they moved to the lower counties of Pennsylvania, now the State of Delaware. From here they moved to Lancaster, Pennsylvania, and in the year 1735 they moved to Virginia, and finally settled near what is now Kernstown. There he gave the land on which was erected the first Presbyterian church west of the Blue Ridge, and here they lived and died. They left a large family. His oldest son, William, joined the Society of Friends and settled in Loudoun County. He had a son, James Hoge, whose son was Isaac Hoge, who married Rachel Schofield, daughter of Mahlon and Ann Neill, his wife; they had children, James, Isaac, Josephine,

where Kernstown now is, gave the lot on which the church stands for the use of the first Presbyterian congregation ever organized in Virginia west of the Blue Ridge. The introduction of the Episcopal Church in Frederick County dates from the organization of the county; but little is heard of either church, vestry, or wardens until after the arrival of Lord Fairfax in 1749. In 1752 a vestry was appointed, consisting of Lord Fairfax, Isaac Perkins, Gabriel Jones, John Hite, Thomas Swearenger, Charles Buck, Robert Lemmon, John Lindsey, John Ashby, James Cromley, and Lewis Neill. Lord Fairfax, in 1752, gave a lot in the southwest corner of the public square in Winchester, upon which shortly afterwards was erected a rude chapel. This was occupied many years, but a better one of stone was reared upon the same spot some years before the Revolution.

"The first settlers were neither distinguished for literature nor religion. They were patient, enterprising men. A true account of their sufferings, their dangers, and their exploits would appear to us like tales of romance. They had not leisure, if they had the ability, to write history. They were much more conversant with the axe, the firelock, and the sword than books and pens. Their children were educated as their surroundings justified,—not for show, but for usefulness. The bravest and best man was the most popular and most respected. Those who possessed a goodly share of book learning could by no means be ignored."

During the summer of 1759 the small-pox broke out in the town of Winchester, and carried many persons to the grave. The court was in consequence moved to Stephensburg for a year. The same dread disease again made its appearance in the years 1771 and 1776, and raged with great fury, spreading over the entire country and among the large number of Hessian prisoners confined in barracks west of the town.

Lewis, William, and Annie. Dr. Robert White married one of the elder William Hoge's daughters, and settled near North Mountain, Frederick County. They had three sons,—viz., John, Robert, and Alexander, the latter the eminent lawyer of Winchester during the Revolution, and a member of the first Congress.

Family Record of William Jolliffe and Phœby, his wife. Married about the year 1720.

William Jolliffe,
James Jolliffe,
Edmund Jolliffe,
John Jolliffe,
and perhaps others.

William Jolliffe, son of Joseph Jolliffe and Ruth, his wife, was born at his father's plantation on the Western Branch of Elizabeth River, Norfolk County, Virginia, about the year 1695.[1] This plantation had been given to Joseph Jolliffe by his father, John, during his lifetime, and was sold by Joseph when he was an old man, and probably his children had all left him to seek homes of their own. William Jolliffe was carefully educated and trained to the profession of law. His father was executor for a number of estates and seems to have had much to do with courts, hence it was but natural he should wish at least one son to follow that profession. At that time lawyers were educated in the law by entering the clerks' offices and acting as deputies, and it would appear that William was so trained. From the time of Bacon's Rebellion until the administration of Governor Spottswood, 1710, Virginia had made but little progress towards settling her vast territories.[2] Williamsburg

---

[1] Family tradition says, "William Jolliffe moved into Frederick County from Eastern Virginia among the earliest settlers; that he was well educated but poor and was seeking to better his fortunes." In the General Land Office at Richmond, Virginia, I find "William Jolliffe Sr. patented 304 acres on the Drains of Babbs Creek, Frederick Co. Surveyed by John Mauzy. John Adams lived on it July 3, 1766." "Wm. Jolliffe Sr 37 acres. Land on which he now lives July 4, 1766." (This was the Red House tract.) "William Jolliffe Sr. 129 acres on Drains of the Opeckon, joins Doster & William Dillon, Survey made to William Jolliffe Jr. and James Jolliffe Nov. 4, 1766." Grant to "William Jolliffe Jr. and James Jolliffe of Frederick County whereon William Jolliffe Sen. lived, joining on Alexander Ross, and being part of his grant," containing five hundred acres "as by survey and Platt thereof made (in behalf of Mr. William Jolliffe Sen.) by Mr. William Baylis." April 7, 1755.

[2] "The first half of the eighteenth century, to the breaking out of the French and Indian War, is extremely barren of incidents in the history of Virginia.

was then the capital, and the inhabited frontiers extended only a few miles north and east of that town. Spottswood was an accomplished and enterprising man, and soon after his appointment as lieutenant-governor of the province began pushing the settlements west and encouraging the people to open up new territory. Immigrants increased in numbers and pushed west. The old settlers caught the spirit of the times, and many sold out their farms and took up better lands in the new counties being formed. Then as now the young men left home and sought their fortunes in the new country. As the territory filled up, new courts were requested and lawyers were in demand, and we find the young men of that profession pressing to the front. Among those who followed this tide was William Jolliffe, who followed the formation of the courts at Spottsylvania, May 1, 1721. (The first court sat on the 1st day of August, 1722, at Germanna.) There was a massacre of the inhabitants of this town shortly after its establishment, "perpetrated by the Indians and sternly revenged by the whites." Hugh Jones, in 1724, thus describes Germanna: "Beyond Colonel Spottswood's furnace, above the Falls of Rappahannock River, within view of the vast mountains, he has founded a town called Germanna, from some Germans sent over by Queen Anne, who are now removed up further. Here he has servants and workmen of most handicraft trades; and he is building a church, courthouse, and dwelling house for himself, and with his servants and negroes he has cleared plantations about it, proposing great encouragement for people to come and settle in that uninhabitated part of the world, lately divided into a county."

Orange County was formed in 1734 from Spottsylvania, and hither William Jolliffe drifted with his family. In 1738 Frederick County was formed, but it was not until October 2, 1743, that Governor Gooch issued an order for the formation of a court upon the petitions of the leading men. At the opening of this court William Jolliffe was among the very first to enroll himself as a lawyer. "On Nov. 11, 1743, the gentlemen named having been notified of their appointment met for the purpose of organizing a court. At this court appeared James Porteus, John Steerman, George Johnston, and John Newport, who desired the privilege of being booked as attorneys, and who upon taking the oath as such were granted

. . . This brevity arises from the fact that it was mainly a time of peace, which usually leaves but little to record of marked interest to the general reader. Again, the annals of Virginia, during this period, are brief and unsatisfactory, and, doubtless, much highly valuable material is, in consequence, forever lost."

the use of the courthouse. On Friday, Jan. 13, at a meeting of the court, five more lawyers placed themselves on the roll of attorneys for Frederick County, they being William Russell, John Quinn, Gabriel Jones, William Jolliffe and Michael Ryan." To a deed given by James Wood, conveying the land on which Winchester was founded, we find his name as one of the three witnesses signed thereto.

Just where he first established his home I am unable to say, but the records of the county show that shortly after this date he was possessed of five hundred acres of land adjoining the lands of Alexander Ross, north of the present town of Winchester. He was from this time until his death in active practice in the courts of Frederick and adjoining counties, his name often appearing in the records. In September, 1752, he brought an action against his brother lawyer, the celebrated but eccentric Gabriel Jones.[1] "Sep. 20, 1743, John Frost deeds to John Millburn a portion of a tract of land patented by Alex. Ross and John Littler Nov. 12, 1735; the witnesses to this were Alex. Ross, Thomas Wilson, John Littler and William Jolliffe." "May 10, 1744, William Jolliffe was witness to a deed from Isaac Pennington to Thomas Colson." "Nov. 16, 1759, as assignee of Geo. Ross he recovered a debt and interest from Feb. 1748–9."

From these and many other records it appears he became the attorney for the Friends settled in that country, and this no doubt had its influence upon his children, and may have been the means of uniting them with that society. William himself, I feel sure, was never a member, Friends deeming it wrong to contend in the courts, and therefore having little use for lawyers except to draw up deeds, etc. "Mar. 26, 1763, William Jolliffe, Sr., brought an action against the celebrated David Crockett who then resided in Frederick County." When he was about twenty-five years of age he married Phœby ——, by whom he had sons William, James, John, and Edmund, and perhaps daughters. There exists no record by which we can determine his wife's family name, nor when she died. This is not surprising when we remember that the country

[1] Gabriel Jones was a son of John and Elizabeth Jones, of Montgomery, North Wales. He was educated in London (April, 1732) at the Blue-coat School, Christ's Hospital, and was there seven years. He then served six years with a lawyer. He came to America, and March 1, 1747, was settled (at Neill's Mill) near Kernstown, Virginia, where he resided twenty-two years. He then moved to what was Augusta County and settled near the present town of Port Republic. He died an old man after the Revolutionary War.

in which he dwelt was new and sparsely settled and the keeping of birth and death records was disregarded; it was many years later before a law was passed compelling such records to be kept. William left no will, but from court records I find he died in the year 1765. (His son William always signed his name William Jolliffe, Jr., during his life. The last record so signed was Wm. Jolliffe, Jr., *vs.* Wm. Crumly, March 6, 1765. Later witnessed a marriage certificate, Aug. 15, 1765, and did not attach the Jr.) He was interred at Hopewell Burying-Ground, in Frederick County, Virginia. His wife died several years before he did, and I believe the later years of his life were spent with his son William at the old Nevill house.

Family tradition says he was a cultured, refined person, fond of good society and people of learning, often neglecting personal advancement for his books and friends. Of his brothers and sisters I have no information (I am inclined to believe there was a John, James, and Joseph), yet the court records of Norfolk County indicate there were others, but give no names by which they may be traced. Unfortunately, the files of these valuable old records are missing between the dates 1719–1730. They no doubt would have supplied many missing links.

Family Record of William Jolliffe and Lydia Hollingsworth, his wife. Married 1750.

John Jolliffe, born June 18, 1751,
Phœby Jolliffe, born December 15, 1752; died when eighteen months old;
Gabriel Jolliffe, born May 19, 1755; died December 22, 1762;
Phœby Jolliffe (second), born February 12, 1758.

William Jolliffe, son of William and Phœby Jolliffe, came with his father and brothers James and Edmund to the valley of Virginia about the year 1743. (Just where his father's home was is uncertain, he being a lawyer practising in the courts east and west of the Blue Ridge. It may have been on a five-hundred-acre tract of land[1] situated near Opecquon Creek, north of the present town of Winchester and adjoining the lands of Alexander Ross,[2] which land was in his possession as late as 1760.) He was born about the year 1720 or 1721, and joined the Friends' Society at an early age. The

---

[1] In Land Office, Richmond, Virginia: "To Mr. William Jolliffe Junr. of Frederick Co. 'a certain Tract of waste and ungranted Land in the said County, whereon he now lives and bounded as by a survey thereof made (on behalf of Lydia Ross, now wife to the said William Jolliffe Junr.) by Mr. William Baylis, as followeth. Beginning at a white oak corner to John Littler, George Ross and John Ross deceased' 210 acres Oct. 4th 1753." "Grant to William Jolliffe Jr. of Frederick Co. 152 acres adjoining Alexander Ross's Patent land, and William Jolliffe Senr. on the Drains of Opeckon. March 11, 1761."

[2] "Alexander Ross resided in Scotland, where his son John was born in 1637, and his grandson John Ross (the son of John) in 1658. The latter moved with his wife and five children to the city of Derby, Ireland, in 1689. He was in the battle of the Boyne." His son Alexander Ross (who probably was born in Scotland) migrated from Ireland and settled in the bounds of Chester Monthly Meeting early in the eighteenth century. In 1706 he married Catherine Chambers, of Chichester, Chester County, Pennsylvania. In 1713 he moved to Haverford, and in 1715 moved back to Chester, and from there went to New Garden Meeting and settled in that portion afterwards cut off to form East Nottingham Meeting in 1730. About the year 1731 he with other Friends obtained from Governor Gooch, of Virginia, a patent for seventy thousand acres of land in the valley of Virginia, which he located north, east, and west of the present town of Winchester. The minutes of East Nottingham Meeting tell of Alexander Ross having a vendue July 16, 1732, which was no doubt for the sale

F. GUTEK

HO EWELL M TING HOUSE

first record[1] we have of him is found upon a single leaf of the old Hopewell Meeting record, all that was saved from the fire which destroyed the meeting-house and the records from the establishment of the Meeting until the year 1759. This minute of the Monthly Meeting bears date second month 4th, 1748 (the original to be found loose between the leaves of the earliest Hopewell records, now in the vault of the Hicksite meeting-house, Baltimore, Maryland.) It was seen and copied bv me, and reads as follows: "Alexander Ross and his son George are appointed to inquire into William Jolliffe's conversation and what else may be needful and prepare a certificate to Middletown Monthly Meeting in Bucks county." "Evan Thomas and William Jolliffe Jr. having transgressed the rules of our Discipline have given in the following paper which the meeting having well considered of and hoping to be the truth from

---

of his effects preparatory to his moving to Virginia. In these records I find Alexander Ross asks for a meeting for worship at Opecquon, March 18, 1734, and such a meeting was granted after due deliberation, November, 1734–35. "Friends were requested to be unanimous in the choice of the place where such meetings were to be held and build their house." The first record we have of Hopewell Meeting is dated July, 1736, Simeon Taylor, clerk. Prior to this meetings were held at Friends' private residences, and marriages were performed at East Nottingham, one hundred and fifty miles away. Alexander Ross fixed his residence near what is now called Ross's Spring, one of the boldest clear cold limestone springs found in Virginia. (The Ross home was afterwards owned by Fayette Washington, a favored nephew of General George Washington.) The meeting-house, built of logs on a hill near this spring from which water was obtained, stood on land granted for that purpose. This house served the early Friends as a place for worship until 1757, when it was destroyed by fire. The present stone meeting-house was then ordered to be built, and was soon finished. In the year 1788 this house was greatly enlarged to accommodate the Quarterly Meeting, then established. Alexander Ross used great diligence in settling his grant of land, large numbers of Friends from Pennsylvania and Maryland coming to him, and many Scotch-Irish Presbyterians also from York and Lancaster Counties, Pennsylvania. These Friends mostly purchased their titles also from the Indians when they claimed the land. Alexander Ross died in 1748, and was buried at Hopewell; his wife died in 1749. They left children, John, married Lydia Hollingsworth; George, whose wife was Frances ——; David, who never married, died September 3, 1748; Mary, married John Littler (will dated August 13, 1748); Catherine, who never married; Lydia, married John Day, April 21, 1733; and Albenah, who married Evan Thomas.

[1] "Aug. 4, 1747, Alexander Ross, William Jolliffe Senr., John Littler and James Wood gave a bond to Morgan Morgan as administrator of Joseph Bryans Estate." "About this time an enterprising man by the name of Alexander Ross obtained a warrant for 100,000 acres of land north and east of Winchester. His surveys extended along the Opecquon Creek and Applepie Ridge. This tract was settled by Friends, and in 1735 they had regular Monthly Meetings."

their hearts have taken as satisfaction. 'We Evan Thomas Jr. and William Jolliffe Jr. both belonging to the Society of the Christian people called Quakers but through carelessness and unwatchfulness have suffered ourselves to be so far overcome with passion and anger which tended to fighting and quarreling with each other, for which action we acknowledge ourselves highly to blame, it being a breach of the known rules of our Discipline and being heartily sorry for it we do hereby publicly condemn the same, hoping with Divine assistance to be more careful and circumspect in our lives and conversation for the time to come.

"EVAN THOMAS JR.
WILLIAM JOLLIFFE JR."

This Evan Thomas, Jr.,[1] was a son of Evan and Catherine Thomas, who came from East Nottingham, Pennsylvania, and settled on lands adjoining the elder William Jolliffe and Alexander Ross. He afterwards married (before the year 1741) Albenah Ross, second daughter of Alexander Ross and sister of John Ross,[2] who married Lydia Hol-

---

[1] Evan Thomas, Jr., married Albenah Ross, youngest daughter of Alexander and Catherine Ross. (His father, Evan Thomas, Sr., moved with his wife Katherine to East Nottingham June 15, 1730; was a son of Samuel Thomas, of Anne Arundel County, Maryland, born 1655, died 1743, married May 15, 1688, Mary, daughter of Francis Hutchins, of Calvert County, Maryland. His father was Philip Thomas, whose wife was Sarah Harrison; came to America from Bristol, England, and settled in Maryland in 1651; he died 1675 and his wife died 1687. His father was Evan Thomas, of Swansea, born 1580 and died 1650.) Evan Thomas, Sr., came to Virginia from East Nottingham, Pennsylvania, with Alexander Ross. He had moved from Goshen, Chester County, Pennsylvania, some years earlier.

[2] John Ross, son of Alexander Ross and Lydia Hollingsworth, both of Opecquon, in Virginia, passed meeting the first time August 18, 1735, at East Nottingham, Cecil County, Maryland. (Nine miles from Elkton the old brick meeting-house, the land, seven acres, given by Penn.) Passed second time September 15, 1735, Josiah Ballinger and Isaac Parkins to see the marriage properly performed.

"John Ross, son of Alexander Ross to Lydia Hollingsworth, daughter of Stephen Hollingsworth, both of Orange County, Virginia, at a public meeting at Hopewell in Orange Co., Va., October 11, 1735. Witnessed by—

"ABRAHAM HOLLINGSWORTH
GEO. HOLLINGSWORTH
JOHN NEILL
and 36 others

ALEXANDER ROSS
KATHERINE ROSS
Ann Hollingsworth
LYDIA HOLLINGSWORTH
MARGARET HOLLINGSWORTH
MARY LITTLER
ALBENAH ROSS
HANNAH HOLLINGSWORTH."

lingsworth, October 11, 1735. This John Ross died 1748. His estate was inventoried by William Barrett, William Jolliffe, Jr., and William Dillon, and sworn before John Neill, Gent. (a brother of Lewis Neill the elder), January 18, 1748–49, Lydia Ross administratrix. Early in September, 1750, William Jolliffe, Jr., married his widow, Lydia Ross (*née* Hollingsworth). She was a daughter of Stephen Hollingsworth and Ann, his wife, a great-grand-daughter of Valentine Hollingsworth, who came to America with William Penn. She was a second cousin of the Lydia Hollingsworth who was then married to Lewis Neill. Lydia (Ross) Jolliffe left children by her first husband,—viz., John Ross, David Ross, born September 18, 1742, Stephen Ross, and Alexander Ross. By her second husband she left children as follows: John Jolliffe, born June 18, 1751; Phœby Jolliffe, born December 15, 1752, who died when eighteen months old; Gabriel Jolliffe (probably named after Gabriel Jones), born May 19, 1755; and Phœby Jolliffe (second of this name), born February 12, 1758. The wife, Lydia Jolliffe, died December 30, 1759, and their son, Gabriel Jolliffe, December 22, 1762. "At a court held in Frederick County, Oct. 3, 1752, William Jolliffe, Jr. and Lydia his wife, guardian to Alexander Ross, orphan of John Ross, deceased, having produced an account of the estate of the said orphan in

---

"David Ross (born 9th mo. 18, 1742) son of John Ross (who was son of Alexander Ross) and *L*ydia Hollingsworth his wife (daughter of Stephen Hollingsworth) to Catherine Thomas a daughter of Enos Thomas Dec. 20th 1770. Witnesses—

"Phœby Thomas	George Ross	Henry Rees
John Thomas	Alexander Ross	Edmund Jolliffe
Alice Thomas	Stephen Ross	John Jolliffe
{ Evan Thomas	and others	Elizabeth Jolliffe."
{ Albenah Thomas		

"Phœby Ross, daughter of David and Catherine (as above), to Johnathan Butcher of Alexandria, son of Johnathan and Ann, Sep. 4, 1806.

"Witnesses—

"Wm Jolliffe	Catherine Ross
Rebecca Jolliffe	David Ross
John Jolliffe	Lydia Ross,
Abel Neill	Johnston Ross
Rachel Neill	Enos Ross."
and others	

"Known in the family as Aunt Phœby Butcher."

"Stephen Ross, son of John and *L*ydia Ross, moved to East Nottingham from Hopewell in 1758, and was apprenticed to his uncle John Day to learn the tanning business."

their hands and solemnly affirmed to the same, they being of the people called Quakers, the same was admitted to record." It seems that both William Jolliffe and his wife were strict members of the Friends' Society, well educated and prosperous, the wife inheriting from her father and first husband large land estates near Hopewell Meeting-House. William Jolliffe was a well-to-do merchant and miller, and possessed several large farms in his own right, acquired by grant from the Crown and Lord Fairfax and by purchase. His home at this time was known as the Red House, standing on a tract of land containing two hundred and thirteen acres, left by him at the time of his decease to his son John. The house stood a few rods south of the great Pennsylvania Highway, or old Indian or Pack-Horse Trail (now the Winchester and Martinsburg Turnpike[1]), six and one-half miles north of Winchester and just east of the Ross Spring Branch (now the Washington Spring Branch). Just west of and across the road stood his mill and storehouse afterwards bought from Colonel John Nevill[2] and rebought from Fairfax. This mill received its power from Ross Spring Branch. This old Red House was a frame structure built by William Jolliffe on solid limestone foundations, with rived clapboards and wrought nails. It was a noted landmark, having been painted a bright red. In the

---

[1] "The old ford one mile below Shepherdstown was known for one hundred and fifty years as the 'Old Pack-Horse Ford.' It was the only crossing-place in the Potomac River for many miles east and west of it. How long it has been used is a matter of conjecture, but it was the great fording-place for the Indians passing north and south long before the white man trod the soil. Here on both sides of the river occurred some of the bloodiest Indian battles. It was here, September 18, 1862, the One Hundred and Eighteenth Regiment of Pennsylvania Volunteers (Corn Exchange) met such a bloody repulse; the river was said to have run black with the floating bodies shot down in mid-stream from the Virginia bank."

[2] "John Neville, a son of Richard and Ann Burroughs, his wife, who was a cousin of Lord Fairfax, was born July 26, 1731, on the head-waters of Ocequon Creek, Virginia (Bull Run). He served in Braddock's War, and at its close settled near Winchester. Was a captain in Dunmore's War, 1774, and on the 7th of August, 1775, marched with his company to Fort Pitt. He was chosen colonel of the Fourth Virginia Regiment during the Revolution, after the promotion of Adam Stephens. He married Winfred Oldham, who was born 1736; both he and his wife died near Pittsburg, Pennsylvania, where they resided the latter part of their lives. Their son Pressly Neville was born September 6, 1755; was a captain in the Eighth Virginia Regiment during the Revolution; married Nancy, daughter of General Daniel Morgan, and both died in Ohio."

John Nevill was a direct descendant of the great Nevill family of England. His ancestors first settled in the county of Isle of Wight, Virginia.

The Right Honourable Thomas Lord Fairfax Baron of Cameron
In that part of Great Britain called Scotland Proprietor of the Northern Neck of Virginia To all to whom this
present Writing shall come sends Greeting — Know ye that for good Causes for and in Consideration of the Composition to
me paid and for the annual Rent herein after reserved I have given granted and confirmed and by these Presents for me my
Heirs and Assigns do give grant and confirm unto William Jolliffe of Frederick County A certain Tract of Waste and
ungranted Land on the Drains of Opeckon in the said County And bounded as by a Survey thereof made by Thomas
Rutherford — Beginning at a Stake by a marked White Oak near and on the West Side of the County Road Corner
to William Jolliffe and John Neavill — Thence along Jolliffe's Lines East One hundred and forty Poles crossing Ross's Spring
Branch to two White Oaks — Thence North Two hundred and six Poles to two Hickories and a Red Oak Sapling Corner
to Jolliffe at [illegible] Thomas's Line — Thence with Thomas's Line N°. 45 E^t. One hundred and sixty Poles to a White Oak —
Thence S^o. 45 W^t. [illegible] Poles crossing a Road to a White Oak Corner to Thomas and John Littler deceased — Thence
along Littler's Line N°. 45 W^t. One hundred and seventy two Poles crossing the said Road to a Hickory Sapling in the Line
and thence S^o. [illegible] W^t. One hundred and thirty one Poles to the Beginning Containing One hundred and thirteen
Acres — Together with all Rights Members and Appurtenances thereunto belonging Royal Mines excepted And a full
Third Part of all Lead Copper Tin Coals Iron Mines and Iron Ore that shall be found thereon — To have and to hold the said One hundred and thirteen Acres of Land together with all Rights Profits and Benefits to the same belonging or in any wise appertaining Except
before excepted — To him the said William Jolliffe his Heirs and Assigns forever — He the said William Jolliffe his
Heirs and Assigns therefore Yielding and Paying to me my Heirs or Assigns or to my Certain Attorney or Attornies Agent or Agents
or to the Certain Attorney or Attornies of my Heirs or Assigns Proprietors of the said Northern Neck Yearly and every Year on the Feast
Day of S^t. Michael the Archangel the Fee Rent of One Shilling Sterling Money for every Fifty Acres of Land hereby granted and so
proportionably for a greater or lesser Quantity — Provided that if the said William Jolliffe his Heirs and Assigns shall not pay the
said reserved annual Rent as aforesaid so that the same or any part thereof shall be behind and unpaid by the Space of two whole Years
after the same shall become due If legally demanded that then it shall and may be Lawful for me my Heirs or Assigns Proprietors as aforesaid my or their Certain Attorney or Attornies Agent or Agents into the above granted Premises to reenter and hold the same
as if this Grant had never passed — Given at my Office in the County of Frederick under my Hand and Seal
Dated this Fifth Day of November In the Seventh Year of His Majesty's King George the Third's Reign A. D. 1766

Register'd In the Proprietor's Office
In Book N. Folio 309

Fairfax

yard was a deep well surrounded by shade trees. A modern frame structure now occupies the site. The old mill has entirely disappeared, though I can well remember it as the stable of our cousin Meredith Jolliffe (just before the Civil War). "At a court held Nov. 9, 1758, William Jolliffe, Jr. was appointed overseer of the road from Cunningham's mill to Robert Mosley's." This was one of the most important roads in the county, extending from Cedar Creek, fifteen miles south of Winchester, to Mosley's, some twenty miles north of Winchester, in what is now Berkley County, embracing the present Valley Turnpike. At that time only persons of position and influence were appointed to such offices. March 26, 1759, he was appointed clerk of the Monthly Meeting of Hopewell, succeeding Jesse Pugh. This Meeting was established about the year 1735–36 in a log house near the present house. This building was destroyed by fire, and with it all the Meeting records, a loss that can never be repaired. "A committee to 'set the minutes in order for recording' was appointed in 1760, who reported that one of the books being lost by accident by fire they could not proceed any farther back than when William Jolliffe was clerk, to wit 26th of Third month 1759." About this time it was deemed necessary to build a new meeting-house, and July 23, 1759, "It was unanimously agreed that the meeting house going to be built be raised to two story high, and augmented three feet wider than was before agreed." This was the present stone house at Hopewell, which in 1788 was enlarged and added to (Abraham Hollingsworth and Lewis Neill working on the walls in person).

At this time Lydia Jolliffe also appears to have acted as clerk of the Monthly Meeting. William Jolliffe continued to be clerk of the Meeting until his death, having filled for a period of eleven years that office during the most energetic and flourishing time of the Society's existence in Frederick County. The minutes were kept by him in a remarkably neat, clear, round hand, and give evidence of a person of culture and education above the average of his day and generation. The very first record in this old book was of a Meeting held at Hopewell Meeting-House March 26, 1759, at which time James Jolliffe, Thomas Babb, Jr., and John Mendinghall were disowned for some breach of the Society's discipline. This James Jolliffe was his brother. I find that at a meeting held November 9, 1759, his brother Edmund Jolliffe requested to be admitted to membership, and one month later, or December 24, 1759, his request was granted. On December 30, 1759, his wife, when about forty-one years old, died, and was buried at Hopewell graveyard. In the deed books of the county at Winchester I find, "November 13, 1751, George Ross transferred about ten acres of land to Isaac Hollingsworth, Evan Thomas, Jr. and Evan Rogers, for building a Quaker meeting house." This embraced the land now used for a graveyard as well as that on which the meeting-house stands. At a meeting held October 6, 1760, I find his step-son Alexander Ross was disowned for marrying out of meeting. "January 14, 1760, this Alexander Ross, son of John Ross, deceased, and grandson of Alexander Ross, deceased, sold to William Jolliffe, Jr. 220 acres of land being part of a tract of 2373 acres granted Alexander Ross their grandsire by patent in Land Office Nov. 12, 1736. Witness—Joseph Lupton, Wm. Neill, Thomas Jones."[1] This land was willed to his son Edmund Jolliffe, and is now owned by our cousin Edward Jolliffe. When about forty years old, April 9, 1761, William Jolliffe was married a second time to Elizabeth Walker, daughter of Abel and Sinah Walker, of Frederick County, Virginia. This lady was born October 8, 1732, and was therefore twenty-nine years of age.

"Whereas William Jolliffe Junior of Opeckon in the County of Frederick and Colony of Virginia and Elizabeth Walker of the Same place Daughter of Abel Walker and Sinah Walker Decd. Having Declared their Intentions of taking each other in Marriage before Several Monthly Meetings of the Christian People called Quakers at Opeckon aforesaid And having Consent of parents and parties concerned their said proposals of Marriage were allowed of by the Said Meeting: Now these are to Certifie whom it may concern that for the full accomplishing their said Intentions Upon the Ninth Day of the fourth Month in the Year One Thousand seven Hundred & Sixty One They the said William Jolliffe and Elizabeth Walker Appeared in a public Assembly of the said people & others met together at their public Meeting house at Opeckon aforesaid And the said William Jolliffe taking the said Elizabeth Walker by the hand Did in a Solemn Manner Openly Declare that he took the said Elizabeth Walker to be his wife promising with Divine Assistance to be unto her a loving & faithful Husband until Death should Separate them or words to that Effect. And then & there in the said Assembly the said Elizabeth Walker Did in like Manner

[1] "March 3, 1766, Geo Ross sold to William Jolliffe Jr (merchant) for £150 two parcels of land on the main Road from William Jolliffe's to Winchester, being part of a greater tract granted Alexander Ross by pattent, containing 64 acres 10 poles. Speaks of a purchase of a Stone House by William Jolliffe from John Neavil Esq. Witnesses John Shelling, Rich Rigg, John Nevill, Thomas Hide."

Openly Declare that she took the said William Jolliffe to be her Husband promising with Divine Assistance to be unto him a Loving & faithful wife until Death should Separate them or words to that Effect. Moreover the said William Jolliffe & Elizabeth Walker she according to the Custom of Marriage Assuming the Name of her Husband as a further Confirmation thereof Have unto these presents set their hands.

"And we whose names are hereunder written being present at the Solemnization of the said Marriage & Subscription in manner aforesaid Have as Witnesses thereunto subscribed our Names the Day & Year above written.

"Esther Wright	William Dillon	William Jolliffe Jun.
Lydia Cunningham	Henry Rees	*Elizabeth Jolliffe*
Albenah Thomas	George Ross	Wm. Jolliffe Senr.
Sarah Milburn	Eduard Beeson	James Jolliffe
Martha Nelson	John Ridgeway	Edmund Jolliffe
	George Cunningham	Abel Walker
	James Stewart	Lewis Walker
	Alexander Ross	Mordecai Walker
	Robert Bull	Mary Campbell
	Thomas Butterfield	Sinah Walker
	Evan Thomas	Margaret Dorster
	Edward Dodd	Hannah Jolliffe."

(Pages 7 and 8, Hopewell Marriage Records.)

She was a member of Friends' Society and a lady of exemplary piety. They had children as follows:

Edmund Jolliffe, born January 15, 1762;
Mary Jolliffe, born May 13, 1763;
Amos Jolliffe, born August 5, 1764;
Lydia Jolliffe, born May 9, 1766;
Elizabeth Jolliffe, born June 16, 1768;
Gulielmo Jolliffe, born September 14, 1770.

This last, a posthumous child, died January 21, 1773, and Edmund Jolliffe died May 8, 1778, when sixteen years old.

William Jolliffe was a member of a committee of Friends appointed to meet other Friends, March 22, 1767, at Curles, below Richmond, to solicit the governor to remit the muster fines charged against Friends in Virginia. The same year he was appointed "to care for the meeting house in the room of David Ross and make the fires one year from Second Month 2nd, and to be allowed 40 shillings." By order of the General Assembly he was ordered as clerk of the meeting, December 7, 1767, to return to General Adam

Stephens a list of all Friends belonging to Hopewell Meeting. "At a meeting held Eighth Month 6th, 1770, Robert Haines was appointed clerk in place of William Jolliffe deceased." During these years he was an active business man, and bought lands all around him from George Ross, Colonel John Nevill, and Lord Fairfax. With the land bought from Colonel Nevill he acquired a large and handsome stuccoed stone house, that formerly stood on the west side of the Great Road a half-mile south of the Red House. This property afterwards belonged to our cousin Meredith Jolliffe; it was wantonly destroyed by fire during the Civil War. Here William Jolliffe and his wife Elizabeth made their home, and it was in this house that some of the exiled Friends of the Revolution were so hospitably entertained by his widow; and here one of their number, the good old Quaker minister John Hunt, died March, 1778, and was buried at Hopewell.[1] After a well-spent, active Christian life filled with good deeds, William Jolliffe died April 18, 1770, when fifty years of age. His remains rest in Hopewell Burying-Ground beside those of his wife Lydia.

His widow Elizabeth Jolliffe survived him thirteen years, and died about the year 1783, aged fifty-one. She was an elder in the Meeting, and was often chosen to represent the Monthly Meeting at the Quarterly Meetings; at that time held alternately at Fairfax, Loudoun County, Virginia, and at Warrington, York County, Pennsylvania. She attended these meetings on horseback though the distance was long, Fairfax being thirty miles from her home and Warrington not less than one hundred and twenty miles. The road to the latter was by the old Indian Trail over the Potomac River at the old Pack-Horse Ford, one mile below Shephardstown, Virginia. It was not until the year 1787 that Quarterly Meetings were established at Hopewell.

---

[1] "A message was sent us from *E.* Jolliffe's that our friend John Hunt, who had been confined to his bed for several days, was much worse; being suddenly seized with a pain in his leg, which rendered it entirely useless, and greatly alarmed the family." "Went out to David Brown's where we received an unfavorable account of John Hunt: mortification had begun in his leg, and made such progress that an amputation of his limb was the only means of arresting it." William Smith rode all night for Dr. General Stephens to perform the operation. The operation was performed the 22d, by Drs. Mackey and Stephens. After the wound was dressed, one of the surgeons remarked to him, "Sir, you have behaved like a hero," to which he mildly replied, "I have endeavored to bear it like a Christian." He died March 31, 1778, at ten o'clock in the morning. He was buried April 2, during a violent rain-storm, in the presence of a very large company of Friends and others.

The personal estate of William Jolliffe was appraised by John Rees, John Smith, Joseph Day, and Edward Beeson, May 7, 1777, at four hundred and eighty-three pounds three shillings. Among the items were his silver watch, two pairs silver buckles, silver snuff-box with tortoise-shell top, gold sleeve-buttons, riding-chair, and one year and eight months' servitude of a man's time, rifles, guns, etc., and sundry books. Elizabeth Jolliffe's personal estate was appraised, September, 1783, by Peter Babb, Jonathan Wright, and Isaac Brown for three hundred and thirty-eight pounds eleven shillings and sixpence. William Jolliffe's will bears date January 15, 1769, with a codicil bearing date January 24, 1770. He disposes of his estates, amounting to eleven hundred acres of land, and orders his other property sold and divided among his children. His negroes he orders shall be set free at their attaining the age of eighteen years.

Family Record of James Jolliffe and Hannah Springer, his wife. Married 1760.

James Jolliffe, son of William and Phœby Jolliffe, came to the valley of Virginia with his father in the early part of the eighteenth century. He early in life joined the Society of Friends, but was disowned March 26, 1759. What the fault was cannot now be determined, though I presume it was for marrying a person not of the Society. The old Meeting records for the twenty-four years from the organization of Hopewell Meeting until 1759 that were destroyed would have given us much information about James Jolliffe. He married in 1760 Hannah, grand-daughter of Dennis Springer, who had a grant of lands from Lord Fairfax, of date November 4, 1754, situated on Back Creek, near Dillon's land, and locally known as the Hog Bottom, because of the abundance of wild pea vines that attracted large droves of wild hogs to the locality.[1] His father William Jolliffe, September 5, 1769, bought of Josiah Springer, father of Hannah Jolliffe, one hundred and seven acres of the above grant and gave it to him. He also had a farm of one hundred and fifty acres of land situated sixty-five miles

---

[1] "James Jolliffe and Hannah, grand-daughter of Dennis and Ann Springer, were married near Winchester, Va., and shortly after moved to near Uniontown, Pa., where he remained up to the time of his death, which occurred about the year 1771. His remains were interred in the Old Cemetery near Uniontown, Pa. His widow subsequently married Charles Harryman about the year 1773, by whom she had one son, Job Harryman, born Feb. 23, 1774. (The record of this family is copied from their Family Bible, which was printed in Edinburgh, Scotland, in the year 1745. Said Bible is now in possession of Oliver P. Jolliffe.) Their children were:

"William Jolliffe, born May 30, 1761.
Ann Jolliffe, born August 15, 1762.
Drew Jolliffe, born September 2, 1764.
Elizabeth Jolliffe, born June 16, 1766.
John Jolliffe, born July 6, 1768.
Margaret Jolliffe, born October 23, 1770.

"It appears from his will that his children, Drew, Elizabeth, and Margaret, were dead when it was drawn, Aug. 27th, 1771. His daughter Ann never married. Of his son John I have no record."

from Winchester (near Uniontown, Pennsylvania, then Redstone), where he resided in 1768, for I find in the court records at Winchester that "James and Edward Bush, deputy sheriffs, paid James Jolliffe 1150 pounds of tobacco for attendance on court 65 miles four times, May 3, 1768."

In his will, after providing for the payment of his debts and funeral charges, he leaves the land he purchased of Josiah Springer, containing one hundred and seven acres, and one hundred and fifty acres surveyed with David Ruble, to be equally divided between his two sons, William and John, his wife to have the furniture and the use of the plantation on which they then reside so long as she remain his widow. He desires his son William and daughter Ann be bound out to learn useful trades. His brother, Sadock Springer, and his wife to execute this will, dated August 2, 1771, and proven November 5, 1771, at Winchester. James Jolliffe and his wife Hannah were both at Hopewell Meeting when his brother William married Elizabeth Walker, April 9, 1761, and they signed the marriage certificate. In the deed books of Frederick County I find that "Aug. 4, 1761, Wm. Jolliffe Jr. and James Jolliffe sold to Innocent Bogoth, John Chennowith and William Chennowith, executors of John Bogoth decd. 500 acres of land formerly owned by Wm. Jolliffe Sr. and adjoining the lands of Alexander Ross Sr. decd. for 220 pounds current money.

		Wm. Jolliffe	[seal]
"Jesse Pugh	*Witness*	Elizabeth Jolliffe	[seal]
Benj. Sutton		James Jolliffe	[seal]
John Cubly		Hannah Jolliffe."	[seal]

This property was at one time in the possession of the father, William Jolliffe. From this deed it appears to have been conveyed by him to his sons, William and James, and by them sold during his lifetime. This, no doubt, was done to provide for his children.

He seems to have been a man of strong religious feeling, and, though not possessed of much of this world's goods, left a fair name behind him. His descendants are very numerous, having settled in West Virginia and Pennsylvania; from there some moved to Ohio and then west.[1]

Of Edmund Jolliffe, son of William and Phœby Jolliffe, we know

[1] See an interesting little publication printed at Morgantown, West Virginia, 1878: "Family Record and Genealogy of the Jolliff Family, from the Year 1760 to 1878 inclusive. By Oliver P. Jolliff and James Watson."

very little. By request he was admitted to the Society of Friends, December 24, 1759. That he continued to be an active member of this people I have every reason to believe. He never married, and died when comparatively a young man. The records of Hopewell Meeting were so carefully kept after 1759 that had he married a record of it would undoubtedly have appeared; nor can I find in the court records anything relating to him. That he commended himself to his brother William is abundantly shown by the fact of his having named a son after him. He was present at the marriage of William Jolliffe to Elizabeth Walker, 1761, and signed the marriage certificate. I am strongly inclined to believe that William and Phœby Jolliffe also had a son, John Jolliffe,[1] who settled on the frontier, in what is now Hampshire County, and that he married and left children, one of whom was a Baptist minister named Abner. The fact that William Jolliffe named his first child John when his father's name was William would seem to indicate that he had a favorite brother bearing that name. James Jolliffe also named one of his sons John.

"Elder Abner Jolliff (born about 1750 or 1751; his father about the year 1725—Ed.), who lived and died in Barren County, Kentucky, was born in Greenbrier County, Virginia, and came of an English family of Norman descent, who settled in Virginia in the seventeenth century; his four sons, Abner, Richard, James, and Elijah, and three daughters, Rachel, Elizabeth, and Jehoida, emigrated to Illinois in the early days and settled in Jefferson, Clinton, Marion, and Washington Counties, where they now have a large number of descendants.

"Abner, the oldest son, in 1824, settled about three miles north of the present town of Richview, Washington County; raised a large family, nearly all now dead; his son Richard was somewhat noted as a Baptist preacher of promise, and died young.

"Richard, the second son, settled the same year near his brother, both being on the old Vincennes trace; raised a large family, and his son Jacob, born on the claim the first year of the sojourn of the family in this State, yet owns and occupies the old homestead, one of the finest farms in Southern Illinois. Elizabeth, his oldest daughter, married an Englishman named Edward Russell; their sons, Thomas and J. K. Russell, are well-known citizens of Wash-

---

[1] "Among the early settlers of Wheeling, Virginia, was a Daniel Jolliffe, whose family were murdered by the Indians and a young son taken prisoner, June 8th, 1792. A probable descendant of John Jolliffe."

ington County. Martha, his second daughter, married Reece Williams and raised a large family, and surviving her husband, now lives in Texas with her children. James E., the oldest son, lives near Fort Scott, and was a soldier in the Mexican War, in Captain Coffee's company of Colonel Bissell's regiment (Second) Illinois Volunteers. Aaron, the second son, lived and died near the old home farm in Washington County; was a soldier in Company C, Fourteenth Regiment United States Infantry, during the Mexican War. His daughter, Mrs. T. B. Affleck, resides in Richview. Abner, the third son, was drowned when a young man, in crossing Grand-Point Creek when the stream was in a swollen condition. Richard, the fourth son, married Elizabeth Taylor, daughter of Press. Taylor, a well-known pioneer of Washington County; was a soldier in the war of the Rebellion, in Company B, Sixty-second Illinois Infantry, and died at Pine Bluff, Arkansas, August 2, 1864. Jacob, the fifth son, the youngest and only surviving member of his father's large family, was born February 5, 1825, on the farm he now lives on and owns, one mile south of Irvington, Washington County, at the crossing of the Illinois Central Railroad over the old Vincennes and Kankaskia trace; married Elizabeth Willard, and has a family of four sons and one daughter, who have all survived their mother.

"Colonel James, the third son, settled about the year 1828 on Crooked Creek, Clinton County, a few miles southwest of the present city of Centralia, and built a water-mill, about 1830, on that stream near the site of Sherwood's horse-mill, erected in 1817; was a Virginia soldier in the War of 1812, and with his brother-in-law, James Rhea, served with Perry on Lake Erie, being among the contingent of one hundred and fifty men furnished by General Harrison to Commodore Perry to complete the crews in his fleet; both were afterwards engaged in the battle of the Thames, September 17, 1813, where the celebrated Indian chief Tecumseh was killed. They were both celebrated Indian-fighters in the early days of the Northwest. Colonel Jolliff was twice married and left numerous descendants. His oldest son was Jackson Jolliff. Reuben W. Jolliff, his second son, was captain of Company G, Eleventh Illinois Infantry, in the war of the Rebellion, his younger brother, Samuel A., being second lieutenant of the same company, who, with his brother Abner, are now living in Patoka, Marion County. Colonel Jolliff's daughter, Elizabeth, married E. Orvis, and lives near the old Jolliff mill in Clinton County, where they have raised a numerous family. Another son, Elijah, served in Company B, Sixty-second Illinois

Volunteer Infantry, in the Rebellion, and died at Pine Bluff, Arkansas, July 28, 1864.

"Elijah, fourth son, settled in Jefferson County in the spring of 1825; had previously married in Kentucky, and had several children; was accidentally killed, Christmas, 1832, at the home of ——, in Jefferson County, by his nephew, Captain James Rhea, a tow wad from a Christmas gun severing the femoral artery. Two of his sons, Randall and William, and his daughter Elizabeth, married to James Willard, live in Oregon County, Missouri. Elijah Jolliff, his third son, lives near Irvington, Washington.

"Rachel, the oldest daughter, born in Greenbrier County, Virginia, October 16, 1783; married November 20, 1801, James Rhea, born in the same county, June 3, 1780; moved to Barren County, Kentucky; had ten children; then moved to Jefferson County, Illinois, to the old Rhea place, four miles northeast of Richview, in 1824, where their youngest child, Thomas F., was born, July 28; in 1827 James Rhea and most of his family moved to Island Grove township, in Sangamon County, where he died in 1843, his widow in 1851. Of their children, the oldest was Elizabeth, born in 1802, in Barren County, Kentucky, and married there to George May; emigrated from thence with their parents first to Jefferson County, then to Sangamon; moved afterwards to Mason County, where she died; her husband and children then moved to Gentry County, Missouri. The oldest son was James, who was born August 27, 1804; married in Jefferson County, Illinois, in 1826, Susan Mattox; was a soldier in Captain Bowman's company in the Black Hawk War; a captain of militia in 1832–33; after killing his uncle accidentally in 1832 moved near Little Rock, Arkansas, in the fall of 1834, and died there in 1840, leaving a widow and three children. William, the second son, born March 10, 1807; married December 11, 1828, Susan Foutch, in Sangamon County; had twelve children, nine of whom lived to maturity; and died February 8, 1860; his widow lives near New Berlin, Illinois. Richard, the third son, born January 14, 1809; married to Eliza Rhea and had three children; when he died his widow married William Etheridge, and moved to Iowa. Jehoida, born October 11, 1813; married, in Sangamon County, John Foutch in 1827, and had four children, and died about fifteen years ago. Rachel died at the age of ten. John, born July 14, 1817; married November, 14, 1839, Julia A. Stark, born June 21, 1823, in Rutland, Vermont; they had seven children, and with their children and descendants, live near New Berlin, Sangamon County. Mahala, born April 25, 1820; married, in Sangamon County, Joseph Pulsifer;

had twin sons, Nevo and Nevi, who are married and live in Gentry County, Missouri; their mother died soon after their birth, and their father disappeared, it is thought was murdered for money while on a business trip to St. Louis. Mary A., born October 27, 1822; died April 28, 1851; married E. R. Alsbury; had one child, Lucinda, who married James Shuff. Thomas F. Rhea, the youngest son, born in Jefferson County; married October 3, 1844, Lucinda Wilcox; has five children living, all daughters; is a stock-raiser and dealer at New Berlin, Sangamon County.

"Elizabeth, second daughter, is a most noted pioneer matron of Southern Illinois; was born in Greenbrier County, Virginia, about 1803, and is now over eighty years of age; was married in Virginia to John Faulkner, a member of the celebrated family of that ilk which has furnished Virginia many able men, one of whom was governor of that State; shortly after their marriage they moved to Kentucky, and afterwards to Illinois, settling near her brothers, Abner and Richard, in 1830, where Mr. Faulkner soon afterwards erected a horse-mill, which furnished the settlers in that region their bread for many a year. This couple raised a numerous and historic family, and the husband and father died in 1853. Mrs. Faulkner still lives with her son Abner on her old homestead, where her family of thirteen were, some of them, born and all raised to maturity. John, the oldest son, was a Baptist preacher, and died young. Catherine, the oldest daughter, married Matthew Pate, and died many years ago; her son, John Pate, of Jefferson County, is a well-known lawyer, who formerly resided at Richview. Richard, the second son, died some years before the war, leaving a family. Aaron also reared a family on Grand-Point, and died some years ago. Elizabeth married L. B. Baldwin, who lived at Irvington, and had raised a large and interesting family, among whom is R. D. Baldwin, a successful farmer of Irvington township. Gilbert, the fourth son, was a soldier in Captain Coffee's Company A, Colonel Bissell's regiment (Second Illinois), in the Mexican War, and now lives near the old homestead in Washington County. Margaret married Meg. Taylor, and lives in Kansas. James, the fifth son, died before the late war; although married he left no descendants; was of large stature, as were all the Faulkner and Jolliff families. Abner, the sixth son, was a soldier in Company B, Sixty-second Illinois Volunteer Infantry, and lives with his family at the old homestead, a mile south of Irvington, on the Illinois Central Railroad, and cares for his aged mother. Alexander, the seventh son, who was first sergeant in Company B, Sixty-second Illinois Volunteer Infantry, in the war of the Rebellion, lives near, and has a wife and several children. Charles J., the youngest son, was also a soldier in the war of the Rebellion, in Company F, Forty-fourth Illinois Infantry, and died since the war. Angeline married Clark W. Mitchell, a soldier in Company B, Sixty-second Illinois Infantry, and with her husband lives near Irvington. Caroline, the youngest daughter, married Jackson Trout, and died a few years since in Irvington, where her husband still resides.

"Jehoida, the youngest daughter, married Enoch Holsclaw in Kentucky, and afterwards removed to Illinois, settling near Mount Vernon, in Jefferson County, from whence they again removed to Clinton County, near the town of Central City, where both died many years ago, leaving numerous descendants."—J. H. G.

Family Record of John Jolliffe and Mary Dragoo, his wife. Married 1774.

John Jolliffe, born February 21, 1775;
William Jolliffe, born September 21, 1776.

John Jolliffe, eldest son of William and Lydia Jolliffe, was born at the Red House, in Frederick County, Virginia, June 18, 1751. His parents were Friends, and he therefore had a birth membership in that Society. When a small boy Braddock's War began and Winchester became a garrison town. From that time until he was twelve years of age war raged along the frontier, and the inhabitants were kept in a state of alarm. From his twelfth to his twenty-second year they enjoyed a profound peace, but were rudely awakened by the breaking out of Dunmore's War, and that county became again the head-quarters of the Virginia troops. In these wars his near neighbors took a prominent part; among them was Colonel John Nevill, who lived during Braddock's War upon an adjoining farm, which he sold to John Jolliffe's father, William, and then moved to the present site of Martinsburg. Colonel Nevill was a captain in Dunmore's War, having raised a company from among his neighbors in this part of the valley. It was not strange, then, that the boys reared in such a community, notwithstanding their peace principles, should have been impressed with a desire to become soldiers and join the armies. John Jolliffe was carefully raised and well educated by his parents, trained as a merchant and merchant miller, and therefore must have been well known to all his neighbors for miles around, the mill and store being for such communities the gathering-place for the citizens to gossip and get the news. That he attended meeting regularly at Hopewell is evinced by his having signed marriage certificates of numerous friends and relations. When he was but eight years of age his mother, Lydia Jolliffe, died, and less than two years later his father married Elizabeth Walker, 1761. This circumstance had much to do with his after-life, depriving him of the personal care of a mother's love and tender sympathy. His father died in 1770, when he was nineteen years old.

When he was not quite twenty years of age the Meeting at Hopewell charged him with having attended a horse-race and fighting, and dealt with him accordingly. For this offence he was disowned March 3, 1772. This document reads as follows:

"Whereas John Jolliffe has been educated in the Christian Religion as a believer in and professed by the people called Quakers, but giving way to a libertine spirit hath suffered himself to be guilty of fighting, and being at a horse race in a public company for which he has been tenderly dealt with by the Overseers and others, but their labor of Love not having the desired effect and he still persisting in his undue liberties, which is quite contrary to the truths of our discipline, we can do no less for the clearing of the truth and discouraging of such liberties than testify against him, the said John Jolliffe, and do hereby disown him to be any longer a member of our Society until he comes to a sense of his disorderly walking and make satisfaction for the same, which that he may is desired on his behalf. Signed in and by order of our monthly meeting of Hopewell held the 3d of the 2nd mo. 1772 by

BENJAMIN THORNBURG,
Clerk."

The spring of the year 1774 he was married by a Methodist minister to a beautiful girl, Mary Dragoo, daughter of Peter Dragoo, who was a farmer of his neighborhood. His father having moved with his family into the property acquired from Colonel Nevill, and he having acquired by will the Red House property, he here fixed his home.

In the court records at Winchester I find, "Aug. 4, 1774, John Jolliffe bought of Conrad Glendon for £100 two horses and one colt, one feather bed and furniture, sundry wagon-makers' tools, one woman's saddle, 100 gallons of rum, all in James Gamell Dowdell's store in Winchester." This was a sheriff's sale, and was no doubt attended by John Jolliffe for the purpose of laying in a supply of house-keeping effects. Dunmore's War had now begun and the country was greatly agitated. Captain Nevill marched with his company, August 7, 1775, to Fort Pitt (Pittsburg). "For more than fifty years the mother country had oppressed her American colonies by iniquitous laws, which exasperated the people and kept them impoverished, respectful protest had been disregarded until the people could bear no more, and from one end of the country to the other were to be heard mutterings of a coming storm.

"In the face of this agitation Parliament passed the famous

Stamp Act, which was hurled into the teeth of the long-suffering colonists. The storm instantly burst forth with a fury that wa then beyond the control of England to abate, and shortly swept away in its rage every vestige of royalty. Men sprang to arms as if by magic."

Among the very first to take up arms were two companies from the lower valley.[1] The captain of one of these was General Daniel Morgan, who started with his company from Winchester, July 14, 1775, to join Washington in front of Boston. Colonel Nevill, returning from Fort Pitt, immediately organized a company of the Fourth Virginia Regiment in Frederick and Berkley Counties. The Virginia convention of 1775, by its Committee of Safety, appointed him captain. John Nevill was promoted December 11, 1777, to be colonel of this regiment, and his son Presly Nevill, a lad of twenty years, was captain in the Eighth Regiment. Among the captains of the Fourth were Andrew Waggoner, William Gibbs, John Steed, Peter Higgins, Robert Higgins, and John Jolliffe, all young men. Robert Higgins afterwards became lieutenant-colonel of the regiment. The uniform worn was a black three-cornered felt hat, a blue cloth coat, red waistcoat, and yellow linsey knee-breeches. These men were at once put into service, and participated in most of the battles of that long war. Early in the year 1776 John Jolliffe seems to have been at home on a furlough, and at that time wrote his will, March 22, 1776, in which he speaks of himself as being in good health. Returning to the army, he was stationed with his regiment at Suffolk, Virginia, until sent with their then colonel, Adam Stephens, to Washington's army before New York. With them he participated in the engagements and skirmishes of the American army during that eventful year. "Throughout the campaign of 1776 an uncommon degree of sickness raged in the American army. Husbandmen, transferred at once from the conveniences of domestic life to the hardships of a field encampment, could not accommodate themselves to the sudden change. The Southern troops sickened from want of salt provisions." "Great difficulty was found in supplying the men with arms, tents, or even suitable hospital accommodations. The system of electing officers

---

[1] "Virginia raised in the beginning of the War, Fifteen Continental regiments of about 800 men, besides three State regiments of regular troops, not subject to be ordered out of the State. Besides these were *L*ee's *L*egion, composed of two companies of cavalry and two of infantry: a regiment of artillery under Col. Harrison; Col. Taylor's and Col. Bland's regiments of cavalry and the corps of horses raised by Col. Nelson."

by ballot among the men prevailed, and many of the officers were inefficient. Discipline was not rigidly enforced, and the terms of enlistment were short. Yet this incoherent ragged army always presented a bold front to the enemy. During the winter movements the soldiers of both armies underwent great hardships. Many of them were without shoes though marching over frozen ground, and each step was marked with blood. There was scarcely a tent in the whole army. To add to their miseries the small-pox broke out in the winter camps around Morristown, New Jersey, and proved mortal to many. Orders were issued to innoculate every one, and as few of them had ever had the small-pox, the innoculation was nearly universal. This reduced the mortality notwithstanding whole regiments were innoculated in a day; and the disorder was rendered so slight that, from the beginning to the end of it, there was not a single day in which if called upon they would not have turned out and fought the British." "Officers and men were quartered among the inhabitants during this terrible time, who were also innoculated by order of the authorities." Among the victims of this dreadful scourge at this time was Captain John Jolliffe, who died in his twenty-sixth year. In his will, which was drawn up before the birth of his second son, William Jolliffe, he makes the following provision. After leaving all his lands to his son John and providing for his wife during her life, he speaks of his unborn child, "not knowing whether it would be a boy or girl," provides for a legacy of four hundred and fifty pounds, to be paid when he or she attained the age of twenty-one, by John Jolliffe; and also leaves one slave to this child. This will was presented to court May 6, 1777, and proved by the oaths of John Reynolds and Thomas Edmondson, two of the witnesses thereto, and William Gibbs and Mary Jolliffe gave bond as executor and executrix. His personal estate was appraised May 26, 1778, by John Littler, Thomas Balwin, and George Bruce. Among the items were the following: "One Regimental Coat and Red wescoat, one Surtoot Coat, one Hunting Shirt, one Regimental Hat, three pair of breeches," etc., together with all kinds of farm and household furniture; also a walnut chest, two square walnut tables, a corner cupboard, one large old chest, copper tea-kettle, two flax wheels, sundry pewter plates, bowls, and such like of the old-time articles we read about and long since discarded. He was evidently fond of hunting, as he also leaves sundry rifles, guns, powder-horns, bullet-moulds, etc., and sixteen horses. The total value was placed at five hundred and ninety-one pounds fourteen shillings and seven pence.

It was not until the spring of 1776 that Congress organized the Continental troops; prior to that time all officers served under the State establishments. To these soldiers the various States offered bounties, extra pay, etc. Virginia was most liberal to her sons in this respect, the Legislature passing various laws on the subject. Possessing vast tracts of wild land in her western territory, she located her military grants in these lands. (Congress also gave liberally of these wild lands. In 1788 four million one hundred and eighty-five thousand acres had been granted.) The heirs of Captain John Jolliffe were given by the State of Virginia for his services a certain tract of first-rate land situate in the Northwestern Territory of the United States, upon the waters of the Scioto River, containing two thousand six hundred and sixty-six and two-thirds acres, which land was located by virtue of a Military Warrant No. 825, and is thus described by the certificate of Richard Anderson, to wit: "August 2nd, 1787: John Jolliffe (Heir) enters $2666\frac{2}{3}$ acres of land a military warrant 'No. 825' on the Sciota River at the first fort above the old Chilicothe Town which Town is about seven miles from a place called Camp Charlotte, to run up the river from the junction 400 poles when reduced to a straight line and from the same beginning 400 poles down the river when reduced to a straight line thence off Westerly with the general course of the same at right angles per quantity."[1] The town of Chillicothe covers this land now.

Captain John Jolliffe[2] left two sons,—John, born February 21,

---

[1] Warrant No. 825 reads as follows:

"COUNCIL CHAMBER, June 14th, 1783.

"I do certify that the Representative of John Jolliffe decd is entitled to the proportion of *L*and allowed a Lieutenant of the Virginia Continental *L*ine for three years' service.

"BENJAMIN HARRISON. THOS. MERRIWEATHER.

"A warrant for $2666\frac{2}{3}$ acres issued to John Jolliffe Heir at Law to John Jolliffe decd June 14th 1783." (Book No. 1, page 163.)

[2] An aged member of the family (Rachel Neill Williams) related to my sister an anecdote of this *C*aptain John Jolliffe. On one occasion he and two of his brother officers rode up to the house of an old woman in the mountains and asked her to get dinner for them. While they were there the old woman showed them some puppies; she went down a trap-door to the cellar and handed them up. As the first was passed they asked its name, and she replied, "Captain," the second the same, and when the third was passed with the same reply, "*C*aptain," they exclaimed, "Why, Mrs. B., do you give all your dogs the same name?" "Oh, any puppy dog can be a captain nowadays," was her rejoinder. They had not perceived the neat little trap into which she was leading them.

1775, and William, born September 21, 1776. The younger was born whilst Captain Jolliffe was in the army, and was never seen by him. He is said to have been a tall, handsome man, with very pleasant manners. His widow, Mary, subsequently married Captain John Steed,[1] of the Fourth Virginia Regiment, a resident of Berkley County. He survived the war a number of years, living on his military grant at Sir John's Run, Hampshire County, Virginia. They had no children. Captain Steed was a Methodist elder during the latter part of his life. He was a personal friend of Captain Jolliffe and also of the eccentric Major-General Charles Lee, who often visited at his house.

---

[1] "Capt. John Stead, a supernumerary of the Fourth Regiment of Virginia, Chesterfield arrangement, Feb. 1, 1781." "In a list of officers for whose Revolutionary Services Virginia Land Warrants were issued prior to Dec. 31, 1784, the following among officers other than Generals and Colonels, viz.: Peter Higgins, Robert Higgins, Samuel Hogg, John Jolliffe, Gabriel Jones, John Steed, &c." (Saffell.)

Family Record of Phœby Jolliffe and Mordecai Yarnell, her husband. Married April 5, 1775.

Phœby Jolliffe, fourth child of William and Lydia Jolliffe, was born at the Red House, Frederick County, Virginia, February 12, 1758. Her sister Phœby died when eighteen months old, and her brother Gabriel when seven years old. She was named after her paternal grandmother. Born a member of the Society of Friends, she was carefully educated in that faith. When only one year old her mother died, and her father married again when she was three years of age. At the age of twelve she lost her father. By both her father and mother she was left independent property. She continued living with her step-mother until her marriage when seventeen years old, April 5, 1775, to Mordecai Yarnell. He was a grandson of Francis Yarnell, who came from England in 1684 and settled in Delaware County, Pennsylvania. "He [Francis Yarnell] was a member of the Society of Friends and a man of great influence in the early colony of Pennsylvania. In 1686 he married Hannah Baker, by whom he had nine children."[1]

Mordecai Yarnell was not a member of the Society of Friends, and for marrying him Phœby Jolliffe was disowned April 5, 1775. In the Hopewell Meeting records I find that Phœby (Jolliffe) Yarnell requested to be reinstated in her membership May 2, 1787,

---

[1] "Francis Yarnell of Stone Creek Head and Hannah Baker were married in 1686, lived some time in Springfield, Chester Co., Pa. He died in 1721 in Willistown, Chester County. Children were, Sarah, born May 28, 1687, married William Askew; John, born Oct. 24, 1688; Peter, born Aug. 20, 1691; Moses, born October, 1692; Francis, born Dec. 24, 1694; Joseph, born May 13, 1697; Amos, born Jan. 28, 1700; Daniel, born July 1, 1703; and Mordecai, born July 11, 1705. Mordecai Yarnell, son of Francis, was a Friends' minister 1731. He resided in Willistown until 1741, when he moved to Philadelphia. He married in 1733 Catherine Meredith, by whom he left Sarah, Ellen, Hannah, and Catherine. In the year 1745 he married for second wife Mary Roberts, and by her had children, Mary, Mordecai Edward, Lydia, Ann, Elizabeth, Peter, Deborah, and Jane. Peter Yarnell, his son, became a noted doctor in the Revolutionary service. He was made an M.D. February, 1779. In the later years of his life he lived in Montgomery Co., Pa., and died in 1798, aged 45. His brother Mordecai as above moved to Virginia, and in 1775 married Phœby Jolliffe and removed to Wheeling, Va., where he died."

and that she was so admitted July 2, 1787; that she removed to the bounds of Crooked Run Meeting above Winchester, May 1, 1789; that she signed the marriage certificate of a number of her friends and relations. In the court records of Winchester I find that Mordecai Yarnell and Phœby, his wife, sold March 8, 1780, two hundred and fifty-five acres of land on Babbs Creek to Thomas Ferrell.[1] After this they moved to Wheeling, West Virginia, and settled. John Yarnell, of Wheeling, writing to his cousin William Jolliffe, January 22, 1807, speaks of the death of his aunt Higgins. He sends the love of his mother, sisters, and brother (Peter). She was then forty-nine years of age. We have no record of her death. She left two sons[2] and several daughters. Her family were prominent people in Wheeling, and several members were soldiers on both sides in the Civil War, serving with their commands in the valley of Virginia, and often visited at the Jolliffe house near Winchester.

Edmund Jolliffe, eldest child of William Jolliffe and Elizabeth Walker, his second wife, was born a member of the Society of Friends January 15, 1762, and died May 8, 1778, when sixteen years of age.

---

1 "Aug. 5, 1777, Aaron Mercer sold to Mordecai Yarnell a tract of land on Babbs Creek, Frederick Co., Virginia, containing 250 acres."

2 Mr. Wetherill, of Philadelphia, told my aunt, Elizabeth J. Sharpless, "that he had in his possession a portrait of John Jolliffe Yarnell, who received a sword from Congress for services in Commodore Decatur's expedition against Algeria, June, 1815." Evidently he was a son of Phœby Jolliffe Yarnell, and she named him after her brother, Captain John Jolliffe of the Revolution.

Family Record of Mary Jolliffe and Robert Higgins, her husband. Married March 7, 1797.

Mary Jolliffe, second child of William Jolliffe and Elizabeth, his wife, was born a member of the Society of Friends, May 13, 1763, at the Nevill House, Frederick County, Virginia. When seven years of age her father died, leaving her by his will to be educated until of age, or she married, when certain property was to be given her as her separate estate. She continued to live with her mother and brother until her thirty-fourth year, when she was married by Rev. Alexander Balmain, an Episcopal minister, to Colonel Robert Higgins, March 7, 1797. Colonel Higgins was born 1744, and when twelve years of age had a narrow escape from capture by Indians. Kercheval tells the story as follows:

"In 1756, while the Indians were lurking about Fort Pleasant, and constantly on the watch to cut off all communication therewith, a lad named Higgins, aged about 12 years, was directed by his mother to go to the spring about a quarter of a mile without the fort, and bring a bucket of water. He complied with much trepidation, and persuaded a companion of his, of about the same age, to accompany him. They repaired to the spring as cautiously as possible, and after filling their buckets, ran with speed towards the fort, Higgins taking the lead. When about half-way to the fort, and Higgins had got about thirty yards before his companion, he heard a scream from the latter, which caused him to increase his speed to the utmost. He reached the fort in safety, while his companion was captured by the Indians, and taken to their settlements, where he remained until the peace, and was then restored. The young Higgins subsequently became the active Capt. Robt. Higgins in our Revolutionary army, and after raising a numerous family in Virginia removed with them to the West."

On the breaking out of the Revolutionary War he and his brother Peter were among the first to raise companies in the valley and join the army. Colonel Higgins was rapidly promoted to the rank of lieutenant-colonel of his regiment, the Fourth Virginia, with which he served with great distinction throughout the war. At one time he was captured and remained a prisoner for more than a year, suffering horribly throughout his entire imprisonment. At the close of the war he was given by Virginia a large military grant of land[1] (four thousand acres) situated near Georgetown, Ohio. After his marriage with Mary Jolliffe he removed to his estates in Ohio. His wife died in the year 1806, when forty-three years of age. They left four children, one of whom married Brigadier-General Thomas L. Hamer, United States army.

General Hamer was a very distinguished lawyer from Ohio, and a member of Congress a number of years. While there he conferred his privilege of sending a boy to West Point, to be educated at the government's expense, upon the son of a neighbor, then residing (1837) in Georgetown; and this boy was none other than the afterwards celebrated Ulysses S. Grant. He also appointed to the United States Naval Academy, at Annapolis, Maryland, the celebrated Admiral Ammen, United States navy. Our uncle John Jolliffe was sent out by his father to practise law in General Hamer's office, and afterwards became his law-partner. General Hamer died while engaged in the Mexican War, and his body was brought to Cincinnati for burial, and lay in state for three days at John Jolliffe's house, he then residing in that city. Mary Jolliffe Yarnell must have died about the year 1806, as a letter from John Yarnell, of January 22, 1807, speaks of her death as a recent event.

---

[1] Warrant No. 1693 reads as follows:

"COUNCIL CHAMBER, Aug. 30th, 1783.

"I do certify that Captain Robert Higgins is entitled to the proportion of Land allowed a Captain of the Continental Line for three years' service.

"THOS. MERRIWEATHER. BENJAMIN HARRISON.

"A warrant for 4000 acres issued to Robert Higgins Aug. 30th, 1783."

"Thomas Higgins was one of the earliest settlers on the Cohongoruton. He lived about four miles from Bath, but was driven hence, and removed to the neighborhood of Gerardstown, in the County of Berkley. After his removal three of his sons were taken off prisoners, and never returned. At the close of Dunmore's War, one of them was seen at Wheeling and asked why he did not come home, since his father had left him a good tract of land. He replied that he did not wish to live with white people; they would always call him Indian, and he had land enough." (Kercheval.) "John Higgins took up 110 acres of land in Prince William County 1741."

Family Record of Amos Jolliffe and Margery Perry, his wife. Married October 16, 1794.

Amos Jolliffe, the third child of William and Elizabeth Jolliffe, was born at Nevill House, Frederick County, Virginia, August 5, 1764. He was reared a Friend, and continued a valuable member in good standing until his marriage. At one time he moved within the bounds of Fairfax Meeting, Loudoun County, but soon came back to Frederick County. Upon the death of his father, when he was six years of age, he was left a fine property, to be paid to him at his coming of age. After the death of his half-brother John and of his own brother Edmund, he as eldest son succeeded to the mill and store of his father. He was evidently very successful, and acquired large estates. I find on the court records at Winchester the following: "November 16, 1791, Amos Jolliffe sold to Joseph Bond, for 2050£ a parcel of land situate on Western side of the Shenandoah River and Opeckon Creek being part of a greater tract of 2373 acres granted by patent to Alexander Ross the 12th Nov. 1735; bounded near Alexander Ross' house, John Micklin's land, John Littler's line and George Ross' being 336 acres; also another tract adjoining the above and William Jolliffe decd. line, 23 acres, and another tract near by of 33 acres of Bryan Bruin containing 198 acres. Also another tract on the line of the Glebe land and joining William Jolliffe and George Ross containing 20 acres." These lands came to him by purchase from John McDonald's widow, and were parts of the original Ross grant.

When thirty years of age he was married (by the Rev. Alexander Balmain, an Episcopal minister), October 16, 1794, to Margery Perry, second daughter of Ignatius Perry, of Frederick County, Virginia. Ignatius Perry was a thrifty farmer and merchant who possessed fine estates near Hopewell, Virginia. His only other child, a daughter, married a McCandless, from whom the several estates in that family near Hopewell came. Amos Jolliffe died about the year 1799, leaving an only son, William Jolliffe, who died when four years of age, February 1, 1800. "Archibald Magill (an eminent lawyer of Winchester) was appointed guardian of William Jolliffe, orphan of Amos Jolliffe decd. He gave security in the sum of

$12,000, Ignatius Perry, his grandfather, relinquishing his right in favor of said Magill." His property reverted to the heirs of his half-brother, John Jolliffe, and by the terms of his will came to his eldest son John Jolliffe. Amos Jolliffe was buried at Hopewell, as was his son William. I can find no record of the death of his wife Margery.

Family Record of Lydia Jolliffe and James Bruce, her husband. Married November 6, 1784.

Lydia Jolliffe, fourth child of William and Elizabeth Jolliffe, was born at the Nevill House, May 9, 1766, a member of Friends' Society. By the provisions of her father's will she was left a separate estate on her coming of age or marriage. When eighteen years old she was married (by Rev. Alexander Balmain, an Episcopal minister) November 6, 1784, to James Bruce, a son of John and Ann Bruce, of Frederick County, Virginia. (John Bruce's will was dated November 4, 1747. He left two sons, James and George, a daughter Ann, and had a brother, James Bruce.) For this marriage Lydia Jolliffe was disowned from Friends' Society. James Bruce was a man of property, his home being at what is now called Brucetown, which was named after his family. They left children, all of whom moved to the West,—a son James, who with his family went to Ohio in 1813; a son George; and daughters Elizabeth Jolliffe, Rachel, and Polly. I think there was also a son John. I have no record of the death of Lydia Bruce or her husband. Their home was always Brucetown, Frederick County, Virginia.

Family Record of Elizabeth Jolliffe and John McAllister, her husband. Married ——.

Elizabeth Jolliffe, fifth child of William and Elizabeth Jolliffe, was born at the Nevill House, June 16, 1768. She was left by her father's will property in her own right, which was to come to her when she married or became of age. When a young lady she married John McAllister, a son of James McAllister, of Berkley County, Virginia, one of the gentlemen trustees for laying out the town of Martinsburg and one of the first justices for Berkley County under the Commonwealth. For this marriage she lost her membership among friends. John McAllister was a highly-educated, well-to-do miller. He built one of the largest and best-appointed brick flouring-mills in Frederick County, which was known as Greenwood Mills (now owned by Charles Wood). He used to send his flour to Alexandria, Virginia, for shipment to Liverpool. The firm of Jolliffe & Brown was his agent. He was a very agreeable man and his wife a charming hostess. They entertained their friends in the lavish and hospitable manner so common among the old-time Virginians, and around their board were often gathered such historical characters as Light-Horse Harry Lee, General John Smith, General Singleton, Major-General Horatio Gates, General Darke, and other prominent leaders of the Revolutionary period.

He sold his possessions in Virginia soon after the War of 1812 (about 1814 or 1815), and with his wife moved to Tennessee and settled at a place he designated as McAllister's Cross-Roads, Montgomery County. He was very eccentric and always kept his coffin ready to receive his body should he die suddenly. At the death of his wife Elizabeth he buried her body on the top of a high mountain overlooking the Tennessee River. This point was afterwards known as "Lookout Point." It overlooks the town of Chattanooga, and was made historic by the battle above the clouds, fought there during the late war.

Elizabeth Jolliffe was a tall, dignified lady, fond of society, witty, and quick at repartee. She was very fond of poetry and left a well-selected library to her niece Elizabeth Jolliffe. She left no children to bear her honored name. She was devoted to her family and friends and kept up an active correspondence with them as long as she lived. I have in my possession several interesting letters from her pen. Her death occurred in Tennessee about the year 1818 or 1819. Her husband was a fine business man, keeping his accounts and writing his letters in a remarkably clear, full hand. Just when he died is unknown, as there is no record.

›cord of John Jolliffe and Frances Helm, h wife. Married March 10, 1807.

fe, of Clear Brook, eldest son of Captain John Jolli
ragoo, his wife, was born at the Red House, Frederi
ginia, February 26, 1775. His father died when
n two years old, and by his will expressly provid
ation. By this will, which was made while his fath
on furlough from the army and before the birth
›n, William, John was left all his lands and propert
his attaining the age of twenty-one; but it was e
d that he was to pay to the then unborn child a lega
dred and fifty pounds. His mother was appoint
When about seven years of age his step-grandmothe
lliffe, died, and her estate was apportioned among t
m he was the first. About this time his mother, Ma
ied as second husband Captain John Steed, who h
›er in the Fourth Continental Virginia Regiment,
nd friend of her first husband. Captain Steed w
State of Virginia for his military services a grant
near St. John's Run, now Morgan County, West V
he seems to have taken up his residence with his wi
children. How long he continued to reside at tl
›ertainly known, nor do we know the exact date of l
death. When twenty-one years of age John Jolli
ossession of his property, which comprised the lan
uired from his father (the Red House property), l
ion of his grandmother's estate, and his portion of l
d's estate, who died unmarried, in all nearly one tho

death of his uncle, Amos Jolliffe, and his only son a
, in 1800, when four years of age, John became t
a large part of his estate, which included the c
his grandfather (the Nevill House). He was also
the pension land of his father in Scioto County, Oh
these he disposed of about this time to a man by t
ze. These lands were taken up by squatters, and we

never recovered by his family. They are now very valuable. At the death of Captain Steed he became virtual owner of all his property. Thus by a combination of very unusual circumstances he came into possession of large tracts of land, slaves, and other property and was one of the wealthiest men of that section of the State.

When thirty-two years old he was married, at Winchester, Virginia, March 10, 1807, by the Rev. Alexander Balmain, to Frances Helm, a daughter of Colonel Meredith Helm,[1] of Bellville Farm, Frederick County, Virginia. His wife at the time of her marriage was twenty years of age, having been born at Bellville Farm June 24, 1787. He bought of his brother William a large stone house on the west side of the Great Road, half a mile north of the Red House. This became his residence, and was called Clear Brook, the name being taken from a small stream that runs through the farm. When the Cumberland Valley Railroad built its line they named a station after this place. In the yard surrounding his house was a small dwelling where his mother resided until her death, November 24, 1834.

John and Frances Jolliffe had nine children,—viz., Meredith Helm, born ——, and married August, 1839, Margaret Hopkins, a daughter of Gerard S. and Dorothy Hopkins,[2] of Baltimore, Maryland. She was born August 26, 1817. Lavinia, born ——, and married Samuel

---

[1] The Helm family is of German origin and came to Virginia from Bucks County, Pennsylvania, where the first immigrant of the name had settled. The family became one of the most influential in the valley of Virginia, and for generations have always been represented by one of the name of Meredith Helm.

"The 23 Nov. 1677 a number of Swedes petitioned the Court for permission to settle together in a town at Westside of the River Delaware just below the Falls in Bucks Co. Penna. Among the names signed to this petition is Israel Helm and 24 others."

[2] Gerard and Margaret Hopkins had children,—

Elizabeth, born November 1, 1703.
Joseph, born September 1, 1706.
Gerard, born January 7, 1709.
Philip, born January 9, 1711.
Samuel, born November 16, 1713.
Rachel, born October 12, 1715.
William, born June 9, 1718.
Johns, born August 30, 1720.
Johns Hopkins married, first, Mary ——, and had—
Ezekiel, born March 11, 1747.
Johns, born May 8, 1751.

He married, second, Elizabeth Thomas, who was born 1738, and was the daughter of Samuel and Mary Snowden Thomas (who was the daughter of Richard and Elizabeth Snowden). They had children,—

Hopkins, of Baltimore, Maryland (who was a brother of Johns Hopkins); William, born ——, who married Catherine Newby, of Clarke County, Virginia; John, born ——, who married Lucy Burwell, of Carter Hall, Clarke County, Virginia, daughter of William Nelson and Mary Brooke Burwell, of "Glenowen," Virginia; Selina, born ——, married William Overall, of Page County, Virginia; Amos, born ——, married, Mary Jones, daughter of the Rev. Alexander Jones, of Clarke County, Virginia; James, born ——, married Ann Overall, of Page County, Virginia; Edward C., born November 29, 1824, and married, 1858, Virginia Page, born October, 1839, a daughter of Dr. Thomas Swann Page, of Berkley County, Virginia, a son of Ann Lee Page, sister of Light-Horse Harry Lee; and Harriet, born ——, who married James Tyson (born August 21, 1816), of Baltimore, Maryland.

Samuel, born February 3, 1759.
Philip, born September 24, 1760.
Richard, born March 2, 1762.
Mary, born May 7, 1764.
Margaret, born February 20, 1766.
Gerard, born October 24, 1769.
Elizabeth, born ——.
Evan, born November 30, 1772.
Ann, born February 26, 1775.
Rachel, born September 7, 1777.

Samuel Hopkins, first son, born 1759, died 1814, married Hannah, daughter of Joseph Janney (a brother of Rachel, who married Lewis Neill) and Hannah Jones. They had children,—

Joseph Janney Hopkins, born 1793, married Elizabeth Schofield, and had four sons.

Johns Hopkins, born 1793, founder of the Johns Hopkins University and Hospital.

Eliza Hopkins, married Nathaniel B. Crenshaw, of Virginia.

Sarah Hopkins, married Richard M. Janney, of Maryland.

Samuel Hopkins, married Lavinia Jolliffe, and had John, Ella, Arundal, and Mahlon.

Margaret Hopkins, married Miles White, of Maryland.

Gerard Thomas Hopkins, fourth son, born October 24, 1769, died 1834, married April 6, 1796, Dorothy, daughter of Roger and Mary Brooke, and had children, Mary, born 1797, married Benjamin Moore; Edward, Dorothy, Elizabeth, Sarah, Thomas, William, Gerard T. (born 1815, married Elizabeth Coates, of Philadelphia, and had Frank N., Bessie, Johns, Gerard, and Roger B.), Margaret (born 1817, married Meredith Jolliffe, and had Thomas H., William H., Elizabeth H., and Fannie J.), Rachel.

Elizabeth Hopkins Jolliffe married (1872) Nathaniel B. Crenshaw, of Virginia, and had Margaret, John Meredith, Nathaniel, and Fannie. Only the two daughters are now living.

John Jolliffe was one of the county justices of Frederick County in the year 1801, and was always therefore styled Squire Jolliffe, or Colonel Jack Jolliffe. He served for a short time during the War of 1812 as a captain, being stationed near Norfolk, Virginia. He was often seen in the streets of Winchester, talking and laughing with the wagon masters and factors who shipped goods to the South over the great Valley Road,[1] Winchester being at that time the great gathering, stopping, and distributing point for the important trade which reached over the entire South. He was a tall, well-built man of striking appearance. He died at Clear Brook, August 2, 1838, aged sixty-four years, and his remains were interred at Hopewell Burying-Ground. His widow lived to be nearly eighty-six years of age, and died at Clear Brook, February 5, 1873. Her remains were placed beside those of her husband in Hopewell Burying-Ground.

Soon after the war the home of John Jolliffe, then in possession of his youngest son, Edward, was destroyed by fire, and with it most of the old family records, which went back to the settlement of Frederick County, A frame building was erected on the site of the old homestead, and here Edward Jolliffe still resides. John Jolliffe's large estates were divided among his children, Meredith, the eldest son, receiving the old Nevill homestead, where he resided until his death in 1858. Soon after this his wife moved with her family to Baltimore. This old house was wantonly destroyed by a Union soldier during the late war. Being unoccupied, he sought its friendly shelter for the night and fired it on leaving in the morning. The property has since been sold, and is no longer held by any of the family. Meredith's property also included the old mill and storehouse, and the site of the old Red House, then destroyed. At the sale of his property these original family holdings and historic landmarks passed into alien hands, and are no longer held by any of the Jolliffe descendants.

Amos Jolliffe received as his portion of his father's estate the

---

[1] "The Wilderness Road," by Colonel Thomas Speed, of Louisville, Kentucky. (Filson Historical Club.)

"Supplies of dry goods, groceries, hardware, etc., were hauled over this route, *via* Winchester, from the South by way of Cumberland Gap, as far west as Nashville, in those picturesque land schooners, or 'Tennessee ships of the line,' the Conestoga wagon, with their high-bowed covers and six-horse teams with jingling bells making music as they went. The drivers of these teams were a hardy, honest, jolly set, who knew and were known by everybody on their route for hundreds of miles. They were trusted and popular all along the Road."

western half of the Clear Brook Farm, lying east of Hopewell Meeting-House. Here he resided until after the war, when he sold out and moved to Maryland. Edward C. Jolliffe holds the eastern half of the Clear Brook Farm, including the home property, and here he and his wife and youngest son reside. William Jolliffe resides with his family in Prince William County, Virginia, where he holds fine grazing lands; some of his children, I believe, reside in California.

James Jolliffe was an officer of the Confederate army, and was killed at the battle of Malvern Hill, Virginia, July 1, 1862. His widow, a very talented woman, edited a church paper in Philadelphia after the close of the late war. They had no children. John Jolliffe and his wife lived and died in Clarke County, Virginia. Their two sons, William and John, are living near Millwood, Clarke County. Both have families.

Meredith Jolliffe and Margaret Hopkins, his wife, had four children: Thomas H., who married, first, the widow of Frank Barlow, of New York, and second, Miss Agnes Blake Williams, daughter of Moses Blake Williams, of Boston, Massachusetts. They reside on Charles River, near Boston. William H. twice married. His second wife was Mary C. Scott, daughter of Hamilton Scott, M.D., of Baltimore, Maryland. He left two daughters at his death, which occurred several years ago. Elizabeth H., who married Nathaniel B. Crenshaw, son of Nathaniel B. Crenshaw, of Richmond, Virginia. They have two surviving children, Margaret and Fanny. Their home is in Philadelphia. Fanny H., who married William Gilmor, son of William Gilmor, of Baltimore, Maryland. She died a few years ago and left no children. She was considered a very beautiful woman. After the death of her sister Elizabeth Hopkins and her daughter Fanny Gilmor, Margaret Jolliffe went to reside with her only daughter, Elizabeth Crenshaw, in Philadelphia.

Lavinia Jolliffe and Samuel Hopkins left four children,—viz., John, who married Betty ——, and resided at the old Hopkins homestead, at West River, Md.; he died some years ago, leaving no children; Arundel, who died in Paris, France, unmarried; Ella, who married Monroe Mercer, of Maryland, and left four children, two sons and two daughters; Mahlon H., who died in Baltimore unmarried.

Harriet Jolliffe, eighth child of John Jolliffe and Frances Helm, his wife, married James Tyson, of Baltimore, Maryland, and left two children,—Frank Tyson, who died some years since in Baltimore unmarried, and a daughter Lily, who married Gaston Manly, a son of

Judge Manly, of the distinguished family of that name, of North Carolina; they reside in Ellicott City, Maryland, and have two children, Elizabeth Brooke Manly and Martha Ellicott Tyson Manly.

Edward C. Jolliffe and Virginia Page have three surviving children,—namely, Thomas Swann Page Jolliffe, married, and living near Baltimore, Maryland; Lily H. Jolliffe, married, first, Rev. Dr. Harris. (Dr. Harris was a minister of the Episcopal Church for many years, and held the highest degree of the Masonic fraternity in America. His grandfather was the principal founder of Harrisburg, Pennsylvania, the town receiving its name from him. His house, still standing, was the residence of the late Simon Cameron.) He died a few years ago, and his widow has since married H. N. Taplin, of Montpelier, Vermont, where they now reside. Frank Tyson Jolliffe, their youngest son, lives with his parents at Clear Brook, Virginia.

Family Record of William Jolliffe and Rebecca Neill, his wife. Married September 12, 1799.

William Jolliffe, of Swarthmore, second son of Captain John Jolliffe and Mary Dragoo, his wife, was born at the Red House, Frederick County, Virginia, September 21, 1776. His father was in the army at the time of his birth and died without ever having seen him. By his will, which was made before the birth of this child, he provided for his education. Having willed all his property to the eldest son, John, he set aside a legacy of four hundred and fifty pounds to be paid him at his attaining the age of twenty-one years. He also left a slave woman called Phillis. The above legacy was paid in the following manner. In the court records at Winchester appears this entry: "Sept. 10, 1798. John Jolliffe sold to William Jolliffe a tract of land being part of the original tract granted by Thos. Lord Fairfax to Wm. Jolliffe Jr. situate and lying etc. Grant of date of Oct. 4, 1753 and willed by him Wm. Jolliffe Jr. to his son John Jolliffe and devised by John Jolliffe to his son John Jolliffe by Will. Evan Thomas and Amos Jolliffe adjoining and containing 50 acres.

JOHN WRIGHT
AMOS JOLLIFFE } *Witnesses.* JOHN JOLLIFFE."

This piece of land was part of the Red House tract.

William Jolliffe lived with his mother at the Red House until her marriage to Captain John Steed, when she and her two sons moved to the military grant of Captain Steed, near St. John's Run, West Virginia. Here they continued to reside until the death of Captain Steed, when his family moved back to Frederick County, Virginia. William was carefully educated; his step-father being an unusually intelligent, well-educated man, and having no children of his own, he, no doubt, had a good influence over his wife's boys. William, when twenty-three years of age, September 12, 1799, was married at Hopewell Meeting-House to Rebecca Neill, daughter of Lewis Neill and Rachel Janney, his wife, of Swarthmore, Virginia. The marriage certificate I have in my possession. Their first home was made in what is now known as Berkley County, Virginia. Here they resided until after the birth of their second child.

William Jolliffe son of John Jolliffe dec'd and Mary his wife, of Frederick county and state of Virginia, and Rebecca Neill Daughter of Lewis Neill and Rachel his wife, of the same place, having declared their intention of Marriage with each Other, before several monthly meetings of the people called Quakers, held at Hopewell, in the county & State aforesaid, and no objection appearing, their said proposals were allow'd off by the said meeting. —— Now these are to certify whom it may concern, that for the full accomplishing their said intention, this Twelveth day of the Ninth month, One Thousand Seven hundred and Ninety Nine, They the said William Jolliffe, and Rebecca Neill, appeared in a public meeting of the said people at Hopewel, And he the said William Jolliffe taking the said Rebecca Neill by the hand, did in a solemn manner Openly declare, that he took her to be his Wife, promising with Divine assistance to be unto her, a loving and faithful Husband, until death should seperate them, and in the same Assembly the said Rebecca Neill, did in like manner declare, that she took him the said William Jolliffe to be her Husband, promising with Divine assistance to be unto him a loving and faithful Wife, until death should seperate them, (or words to the same import) And moreover they the said William Jolliffe and Rebecca (she according to the custom of marriage assuming the Name of her Husband) as a full confirmation thereof, and in Testimony thereto, did then and there to these presents set there Hands. ——

William Jolliffe
Rebecca Jolliffe

We who were present among others at the above Marriage, have also subscribed our Names, as Witnesses thereto, the day and year aforesaid - - - - - - -

Cuthbert Hayhurst
Thomas Neill
Mary Neill
Thomas Neill
Joseph Neill

Samuel Jones
Abel Walker jun
Isaac Walker Jun
Robert Bond
David Ross
Joseph Bond
Elizabeth Bond
Saml McPherson
Samuel Miller
Lewis Neill
Wm H Brown
Daniel McPherson
Joseph Lupton
Isaac Neill
Joseph Steer Junr

Richd Ridgway
Jonas Steere
Lewis Walker
Abel Walker
Mord Walker
Abraham Branson
Isaac Smith
David Ross jun
Isaac Hewitt
Edward Walker
Joseph Steer
John Cowgill
Nathan Littler
John Lupton
Samuel Bond

Rachel Hollingsworth
Charity Ridgway
Mary Walker
Hannah Lambourn
Mary Ross
Parmenas Lambourn
Hester Spackman
Ruth Lupton
Mary Steer
Lydia Neill
Ruth Neill
Cassandra Brown
Eliza J Bruce

Lewis Neill
Rachel Neill
Ann Lupton
Phebe Yarnall
John Jolliffe
Lydia Bruce
Sarah Neill
Rebecca Neill junr
Lydia Neill junr
Eliza McAlester
Ann Neill
Mary Yarnall
Thamzin McPherson
Mary McPherson
John McAleston

William was not a member of the Society of Friends, but joined that body for the express purpose, as he declared to Friend Abram Branson, of getting his wife. This old Friend was very kind to him, and cautioned him about so publicly declaring himself until he had been admitted. He was admitted April 1, 1799, after the usual inquiries into his conduct and conversation, and he continued a consistent member as long as he lived. His wife Rebecca was born in the year 1777, and was twenty-two years old when she married. (This year was known as the bloody year, or year of three sevens, in consequence of the many Indian scalping-parties roaming along the border country unchecked, most of the able-bodied men being in the Revolutionary army.)

William and Rebecca Jolliffe had six children, as follows: Lewis Neill, born May 20, 1800, and died October 5, 1804, of lockjaw, from a wound in the foot; Mary, born September 16, 1801, and married Joel Brown; John, born October 30, 1804, and married Synthelia McClure; Elizabeth McAllister, born October 12, 1806, and married Townsend Sharpless, of Philadelphia; William, born February 3, 1810, and married Mary Ann Branham, of Ohio; Joseph Neill, born April 10, 1813, and married Sarah Janney, of Loudoun County, Virginia.

Very soon after his marriage William Jolliffe moved to Alexandria, Virginia, and went into the mercantile and shipping business with his brother-in-law, William H. Brown, a son of Isaac Brown, of Frederick County, Virginia. They ran a line of sail vessels to Liverpool, England, carrying over flour, flaxseed, beeswax, tallow, dried fruits, etc., and bringing back sugar, coffee, tea, salt fish, dry-goods, etc. Sometimes one or the other of the firm would go over as a factor with a cargo.

One of their ships was called the "Diana," and once they had an old cat in the house which was giving a great deal of trouble, and yet no one wanted to kill her. Uncle Billy Brown, as he was called in the family, suggested that they send her to Liverpool in the "Diana," then about to sail. So the cat embarked on what was in those days a long sailing voyage, and they all thought they had seen the last of her. But the first passenger to step on shore on the return trip was the same old cat. Our cousins, the Browns, have in their possession a beautiful set of china in perfect condition which was brought over in one of these return trips. The "Diana" played quite a part in their family history. When the British took the town and seized their vessels the old ship was knocking about the harbor, having been loosened from her moorings. They ordered

Uncle Billy Brown to rig her up for their use, to which he replied, "I own a dwelling and part of a warehouse in the town, but I will see them both razed to the ground before I will do it," thus vindicating his Quaker principles, and neither his person nor his dwelling were disturbed.

William Jolliffe prospered in business until the British occupation of the harbor of Alexandria during the War of 1812, when he and his partner with others were forced to leave, and their shipping was burned or taken by the enemy, and their business utterly ruined. His family fled for protection to the house of his wife's father, Lewis Neill, in Frederick County, when the British threatened to burn the town. After the British departed he gathered up the few goods left and put them in the hands of Mahlon Schofield to dispose of as best he could, and left Alexandria to join his family in Frederick County.

After this disaster to his fortune he continued to reside at Swarthmore, Frederick County, Virginia, until his death. Swarthmore was a good estate of five hundred or six hundred acres of land, on which was a stone grist-mill. Part of this land was inherited by Rebecca Jolliffe at the death of her father, Lewis Neill. The old house was a frame structure, built about the year 1750, to which an addition was built of blue limestone about the year 1800. These buildings are still standing, and are now occupied by Joseph N. Jolliffe, the youngest son of William. William Jolliffe exchanged a portion of his father's military grant in Scioto County, Ohio, for lands in Fairfax County, Virginia. In the year 1829 he exchanged this Fairfax land for a large tract of wild land in Athens County, Ohio, which he devised by will to his children. He visited these lands during the latter years of his life on horseback.

In appearance William Jolliffe was a tall, dignified man, noted for his great kindness of heart. Although a passionate man by nature he seldom allowed his temper to overcome him. He was very particular about his dress, being always neatly but unobtrusively attired. He had a host of friends and acquaintances, by whom he was greatly beloved and respected. At his death, which occurred June 30, 1846, beautiful and touching obituary notices appeared in the leading papers of the State, particularly in those of Alexandria and Winchester. His remains were interred at Hopewell Burying-Ground. "April 1st, 1799, William Jolliffe set free his negroes Phillis, Maria, and Grace and her two children." His widow survived him fourteen years, and died when eighty-three years of age, December, 1860. She was a very remarkable woman, had a wonderful memory for names and dates, possessed a strong constitution, great energy, personal push, and will. She was extremely fond of company, and was thought a very agreeable woman. Born in the midst of the great war for the nation's liberty, suffering terribly by the War of 1812, she died at the very threshold of the civil conflict, but not until she had tasted deeply of its bitter cup. She was the connecting link binding together the members of her large family and numerous kindred and friends. In her house they often gathered from far and near, and all felt it a high privilege and bounden duty to do her homage. Civil war, time, and circumstances have wrought great changes since her death in the fortunes and unity of this family,—so many are dead, and her children and grandchildren are scattered. She retained a large amount of physical vigor and mental clearness to the end. Her step was elastic, her figure erect, complexion clear and healthy, though her hair was white as snow. When over seventy years of age she had the misfortune on two separate occasions to break her forearm, and was in consequence somewhat crippled in those members. Her son John sent her in her old age a pair of gold spectacles, which she thought a great deal of, and which, though constantly getting lost, still came back to her, often from the most impossible places, though more often still, when the household had been thrown into a state of commotion, they were found calmly reposing on the top of her head. Her only surviving child, Joseph N. Jolliffe, now has these glasses. She inherited quite a good deal of silver and English plate on copper from her father and mother, Lewis and Rachel Neill. A silver cream-pitcher and most of her small silver she willed to her eldest daughter, Mary J. Brown. She had also an uncommonly beautiful chocolate-pot of English plate, very tall and of urnlike shape with ebony handle, which went to her grand-daughter, Susan B. Hoge; a large silver soup-ladle went to her son John, and from his widow to my sister, Elizabeth A. Jolliffe. She also gave her niece, Rachel Neill Williams, two very old and quaint pieces of silver, inherited from the elder Lewis Neill, and she said she gave them to her because her mother was called after his wife, Lydia Hollingsworth. One was a pair of tongs of scissors shape with jointed handles, so often reproduced at the present time, and the other was a mote-spoon with short handle and broad bowl, similar in shape to the bonbon-spoons used nowadays. The bowl, however, was perforated with small openings, and it was used in colonial times, grandmother said, to skim the motes off the Bohea tea, then introduced into the colonies. She also inherited the Hessian spoon given her mother, and now owned by my sister, Elizabeth A. Jolliffe; also sundry silver buckles, sleeve-buttons, etc., and various other articles of silver in the possession of different members of the family. When seventy-five years of age she rode her saddle-horse "old Ginny" to meetings and elsewhere, though her usual method of going about was in a big, heavy family carriage that would hold six people, the horses equipped with heavy brass-mounted harness. The carriage was lined with gray cloth, having large tassels inside. She used to sit on her stiff high-backed split-bottomed chair on the front porch of her house and talk with her friends and neighbors, remembering well the dates of all interesting occurrences for years back, her hands meanwhile never idle, but busily occupied with knitting-needles. When a very old woman, one cold winter night when the snow was heavy on the ground, the house was discovered to be on fire, it having originated in her bedroom. Springing from her bed she was the first to give the alarm, and began work in earnest to subdue the flames. The danger was so great that it was deemed best to send the children off to old colored mammy Eliza Allen's cabin. The smoke was so dense that servant after servant was driven out of the room, several of them fainting. The cold was so intense that the water froze on the clothing of those engaged in carrying it. Our grandmother, clad only in such clothing as she had on in her bed, stood in the room directing the workers, and herself pouring on the cold water and snow brought by the household. After hours of such exposure and excitement the house was saved, due largely to her indomitable energy and courage. A slight cold was the only ill effect she felt from this exposure.

By her will, which was dated May 5, 1860, she left her property as follows: Her farm in Clarke County, Virginia, to her son, Joseph N. Jolliffe; Swarthmore Farm to Joseph N. Jolliffe and Elizabeth J. Sharpless. Legacies in money to be paid her son, John Jolliffe, and Mary J. Brown; a legacy for life to be paid her daughter-in-law, Mary A. Jolliffe, and at her death to go to her two children, William and Elizabeth. She provided a home for her faithful old servant, Eliza Allen (known to us as Mammy Allen); Joseph N. Jolliffe to execute this will, which was probated December 31, 1860.

SWARTHMORE FREDERICK CO, VIRGINIA

Built 1750.

OLD PARRY HOMESTEAD, NEW HOPE, PENNA.

Built 1784

Family Record of Mary Jolliffe and Joel Brown, her husband. Married 1822.

Mary Jolliffe, second child of William Jolliffe and Rebecca Neill, his wife, was born at her father's home in Berkley County, Virginia, September 16, 1801. She lived with her parents at Alexandria, Virginia, until after the War of 1812, when she moved to Frederick County, Virginia. She was sent to the school of Samuel Hilles, Wilmington, Delaware, to be educated. When twenty years of age, in 1822, she was married to Joel Brown, a son of Thomas Brown,[1] of Frederick County, Virginia. (His home was what is known as the Clevinger Farm.) Eight years (1830) after this they moved to near Minger Station, Champaign County, Ohio, where they resided the remainder of their lives. They had children as follows: Cecelia, born August 20, 1823; William Henry, born December 25, 1825; Herman Winston, born January 9, 1820; Edwin, born September 14, 1829; Virginia Elizabeth, born March 24, 1832;

---

[1] Thomas Brown was a son of Thomas and Mary (White) Brown, of Frederick County, Virginia.

"Thomas Brown, son of Daniel and Susanna Brown, to Mary White, daughter of Nathaniel and Mary White, at Hopewell Meeting-House, Nov. 17th, 1774.

"Witnesses—
David Brown
Isaac Brown
Daniel Brown
Mary Brown
and others."

These were all his brothers and sister.

Daniel Brown (father of this Thomas) and Susanna, his wife, and their children came to the valley of Virginia from Chester County, Pennsylvania, early in the year 1774.

"David Brown, son of Thomas and Mary (White) (and brother of Joel) of Frederick Co., Virginia, to Esther Wood, daughter of Joseph and Ann Wood of the same County, at Hopewell Meeting-House, Nov. 10th, 1813.

"Witnesses—
David Brown Sr.
Mary Brown Sr.
Joel Brown
Deborah Brown."
and others.

Joel Brown, born May 19, 1835; and Rebecca Ann, born and died November 10, 1839.

Of these children, William Henry died October 2, 1826; Herman Winston died October 13, 1828; Joel died January 19, 1837; Cecelia married Thomas Miller, who died March 24, 1852, and left three daughters; Virginia Elizabeth married Samuel Carroll and had children, Gertrude, Maria, Harvey Bruce, and Shirley; Edwin married ——, and had Marshall R., Robert Emmett, and Charles; Mary Jolliffe Brown died in 1885, when in her eighty-fourth year, and her husband survived her a few years. Both were buried in Ohio. Of their children and grandchildren I know little except that some of them are married and have families living in Chicago, Minnesota, and Ohio.

Mary Jolliffe Brown was considered in the family to have a very lovely disposition, and all through her life was remarkable for her unselfishness.

JOHN JOLLIFFE.

Born, October 30th, 1804.
Died, March 30th, 1868.

Family Record of John Jolliffe and Synthelia McClure, his wife. Married September 23, 1835.

John Jolliffe, third child of William Jolliffe and Rebecca Neill, his wife, was born October 30, 1804, at Red House, Frederick County, Virginia. He was with his father's family at Alexandria, Virginia, until driven back to Frederick County by the British under Admiral Sir George Cockburn in 1814. He received a good common-school education at private schools in Virginia, and, much against his mother's wishes, resolved to study law. These studies he pursued with the greatest diligence when a mere school-boy, often reading late at night before a big wood fire, after all the family had retired to rest. When still a lad he entered the law class of Hon. St. George Tucker in Winchester, Virginia, and had as classmates such eminent men as Hon. Charles James Faulkner, Hon. Fenton Mercer, and ex-Governor John A. Wise. From this class he was graduated and admitted to the bar as a practising lawyer. He at once (1825) resolved to go to the then rapidly filling-up West as offering the best prospects for an active young man to push to the front. He had relatives in the family of Colonel Robert Higgins, settled in Clermont County, Ohio, and in Batavia, the county-seat, he in the year 1830 established his office. He very soon became a partner of General Thomas L. Hamer, and in a few years was elected prosecuting attorney for his county (from the year 1833 to 1837 and from 1839 to 1841). He was an able attorney with a large practice, and was often associated about this time with Governor Salmon P. Chase in resisting the famous "Fugitive Slave Law." In early life he was a pronounced Jacksonian Democrat. While living at Batavia he married, September 23, 1835, a lady from Clermont County, Ohio, Synthelia McClure (daughter of Richard and Catherine), who was born February 19, 1813. They never had any children. Finding that the courts of Brown and Clermont Counties were prejudiced against him because of his very pronounced antislavery views, he dissolved his partnership with General Hamer and in the year 1841 moved to Cincinnati, Ohio. Here he soon won a very lucrative practice and acquired a high place in public estimation as a close debater, finished orator, and earnest philanthropist. He was a warm-hearted, generous, trustful man of broad and enlightened views, always ready to spend or be spent for those in distress or want. His earnest advocacy of the cause of the fugitive slave, together with some bad investments, dissipated his fortune, and the Civil War found him stripped of all save his great talent and standing as a lawyer. Selling house and property he resolved to move to Washington City, where he was largely instrumental in getting established the United States Court of Claims. Here he espoused the cause of the oppressed and wronged men who had risked their all in the Southern cause and lost. His eloquence, ability, and industry as a lawyer and his intimate acquaintance with the prominent men of the then dominant political party secured for his clients advantages they were not slow to recognize. In consequence his practice grew rapidly in volume and importance, and had his life been spared he would more than have recovered his former fortune. The building adjoining his office caught fire and his quarters were drenched with water by the city fire-engines. Standing in this damp room trying to save his valuable papers brought on a severe illness that speedily terminated his useful life at four o'clock the afternoon of Saturday, March 30, 1868. At his own request his body was taken to Hopewell Burying-Ground in Virginia and laid beside relatives who had gone before him. Prompt action was taken and eulogistic resolutions passed by the Cincinnati, Clermont County, Ohio, and Washington City bar associations.[1]

---

[1] "Finding that prejudice engendered by his antislavery course had infected even the judges of the courts of Clermont and Brown Counties, to the prejudice of his clients, Mr. Jolliffe about the year 1841 moved to Cincinnati. A change of residence brought no change of principles. In every possible way he showed his detestation of slavery. In the management of fugitive slave cases he made himself prominent. All hours of the day or night, whether sick or well, busy or idle, the runaway slaves' lawyer was ready to serve his poverty-stricken and forlorn clients, and this without money and without price. In this way his name became associated with some of the most famous slave cases ever heard in our courts.

"He was the counsel of the man Lewis, who was so mysteriously spirited away from the court-room during the trial of Wash. McCreary and Margaret Garner.

"Holding as he did that the Constitution was an antislavery document, he was nowhere more at home than when demonstrating the illegality as well as the immorality of slavery, and all the enactments meant to uphold it.

"Few who heard it will forget his thrilling eloquence when, in the case of certain persons who had been brought into the court-room chained and handcuffed, he demanded that their fetters should be removed and they be treated as freemen until proved to be slaves. In the Margaret Garner case, the commissioner,

John Jolliffe was not a member of any church, but during the later years of his life, while residing in Washington, often attended Friends' Meeting, the simplicity of their worship seeming to attract and comfort him as none other did. He was a diligent student as long as he lived, and found time amidst his numerous law cases to study general literature, Biblical lore, Latin, Greek, Hebrew, French, and German. He was also the author of several books that had a wide circulation during the war. His widow continued to reside in Washington until her death, in March, 1890, and was buried in Hopewell Burying-Ground in Frederick County, Virginia. She was a member of the Baptist Church, a lovely Christian, and left a large number of friends to mourn her loss. Her brother, Commodore R. McClure, of Goshen, Ohio, was in the United States navy during the late war.

---

although he had prejudged the case in advance, as was the custom, could not bring himself to give his decision in favor of the claimant Gaines until an adjournment of the court had permitted the excitement caused by his eloquent plea to subside."

Family Record of Elizabeth McAllister Jolliffe and Townsend Sharpless, her husband. Married 1859.

Elizabeth McAllister Jolliffe, fourth child of William Jolliffe and Rebecca Neill, his wife, was born at Alexandria, Virginia, October 12, 1806. She was named after her aunt Elizabeth McAllister, and was well educated, at one time attending the school of John Pierpont, a celebrated teacher of Frederick County, Virginia. Her home after the War of 1812 was with her parents at Swarthmore, in Frederick County, Virginia. When a young lady she was quite gay and fond of society. In conjunction with her cousins Lavinia and Harriet Jolliffe, Elizabeth and Ann Schofield, her friend Ann Severs, and other young ladies of the neighborhood, many a madcap enterprise was planned and carried out, astounding the old people and amusing the young. This bevy of wild young ladies would frequently determine to have a good time, often at the expense of some bashful beau or would-be suitor. Amidst all this fun and frolic she suddenly sobered down and became a very earnest Christian member of the Society of Friends, feeling it a duty, though a great cross, to adopt the plain dress of the Society. This change in her life drove off a few of her old admirers, but added many more of a very different character. In 1859, when in her fifty-third year, she married Townsend Sharpless, of Philadelphia, who had been told of the "sweet Quakeress of the Valley" by his sister in Baltimore. Her husband took her to Europe for an extended bridal trip, which lasted nearly a year. How she enjoyed and appreciated what she then saw those whose privilege it was to hear her tell it over can testify. Upon their return they fixed their town residence at No. 1209 Arch Street, Philadelphia, and her husband built a beautiful country home at Chelton Hills, Montgomery County, Pennsylvania. Between these homes, surrounded by his large family and numerous friends who were devoted to her, she spent a quiet life until his death, in December, 1863. At the death of her brother William, in 1852, she adopted his daughter Elizabeth, who always resided with her. She continued to live in Philadelphia, living at various times at 1315 Filbert Street, 1017 Clinton Street, and 1434 South Penn Square. She was a great advocate of a thorough education, and aided all she could in the education of her nieces and nephews, having the greatest sympathy for the losses and privations they endured during the war. She was a remarkably well-informed person, an appreciative reader of history and biography, and a great lover of good poetry. She possessed the sweetest of dispositions, great refinement of manner, and was altogether a lovely character, whose society was much sought. After a long and lingering illness, patiently borne, she departed this life March 16, 1883, and was buried beside her husband, in Friends' Burying-Ground, West Philadelphia.

Family Record of William Jolliffe and Mary Ann Branham, his wife. Married 1836.

William Jolliffe, fifth child of William Jolliffe and Rebecca Neill, his wife, of Swarthmore, Frederick County, Virginia, was born at Alexandria, Virginia, February 3, 1810. He was but two years of age when his mother was forced to remove her family to Frederick County, where he was educated in the private schools of the county (their excellency has before been alluded to), having at one time John Pierpont as teacher. He was not a strong or robust child, and it was deemed best to educate him for some less laborious business than farming. His mother determined to have him become a merchant, though his constitution and temperament utterly unfitted him for such a life. When about twenty years of age, in 1830, he began business on his own account at Newtown, Frederick County. Being fond of society, full of life and spirit, and surrounded by young men of means, who led comparatively idle lives, it is not surprising his business did not prosper as it should. In the year 1833, therefore, it was determined he should move his store to Snicker's Ferry, on the Shenandoah River, in Clarke County. This was in every way an unwise proceeding, and after a trial of about a year was abandoned. The goods were brought to Swarthmore in 1834 and disposed of by 1835. The store was kept in a log building situated on the edge of the orchard, and was known as the Storehouse, having formerly been used for that purpose, when the old stone grist-mill was in operation thirty or forty years previous. In the fall of 1835 William went out to Ohio, having secured a position with a man by the name of Crew, in Richmond, Jefferson County. In a letter to his father of date September 30, 1835, he speaks of "having arrived on yesterday at eleven o'clock, left Wheeling Monday, on the steamboat 'Post-Boy,' and went to Steubenville, reaching there at two o'clock in the night;" says he has a bad cold. In Wheeling he visited his cousin, Peter Yarnell, a son of his aunt, Phœbe Yarnell. On the stage he says he met with "friends in the persons of Mrs. Moreland, C. F. Mercer, and Miss Ann Fitzgerald and her mother," adding, "she is a very pretty and interesting girl, and quite intelligent." He thinks he

WILLIAM JOLLIFFE.

Born February 3rd, 1810.
Died March 22nd, 1852.

will be pleased with his new position. At Richmond he was placed in charge of quite a large store, and he also kept the post-office for the village, which he says then contained a population of about four hundred, surrounded by a thickly-settled, prosperous farming community. In a second interesting letter of date November 9, 1835, he tells his father his life at Crew's home, what he does and what he reads; gives prices of all sorts of commodities, and says "lands are worth from twelve to forty dollars per acre." He tells him the salary he is to receive; as an experiment he will stay three months, and if not paid more will quit. It would seem the increase did not come, for about the year 1836 we find him visiting his sister, Mary Brown, at Mingo, Champaign County, Ohio. In that neighborhood there was then living with her adopted mother, Sarah Canby (a first-cousin of his mother, Rebecca Jolliffe), a very pretty and attractive young lady, Mary Ann Branham. An intimacy sprang up between the two which speedily culminated in a marriage, which took place at the home of Sarah Canby in the fall of the year 1836.

Mary Ann Branham was born in Powhatan County, Virginia, in the summer of 1820, and was therefore only sixteen years of age when she married. They had eight children,—namely, Caroline Marcella, William Henry, John Joseph, Elizabeth Ann, Lewis Neill, William, Rebecca, and Mary. Of these only two, Elizabeth Ann and William, are living; all the others died in infancy.

After a visit to his father's home in Virginia, William Jolliffe moved with his wife and old colored servants, Alfred Dixon and his wife, to Snow Fork, Athens County, Ohio, on the two thousand acres of coal land owned by his father. This land was not then cleared, and the country very sparsely settled by a rough population. He placed his family in the home of one of these neighbors while he and old Alfred went vigorously to work clearing off a piece of land and building a house. It was nearly a year before they were ready to move into their new home. During the winter of 1838 William taught a school in the neighborhood. The spring found him busily engaged in planting a crop, felling trees, preparing a garden, and adding to the conveniences of his home; his young wife was in the mean time busy with household duties. She has often told me the country was such a wilderness that both deer and wild turkeys would come up to her door and be fed from her hand. Their neighbors were a rough lot of squatters that gave them much trouble. In one of his letters to his father he speaks of the "impossibility of raising or keeping anything that his neighbors would not help themselves to." Hard work and daily anxiety, the loss of three children, and other troubles, so completely impaired his constitution, never very robust, that he was compelled to give up and move his family back to Virginia in 1841. That journey was an eventful one, travelling for miles through dense forests and deadened timber. They were overtaken by a terrible storm of wind, rain, and hail, trees were uprooted and fell around them, blocking the mountain roads. The streams were swollen and dangerous, and for nearly one hundred miles they were compelled to force their way in the face of danger by unremitting toil. This exhausting trip permanently injured his health.

His father was now an old man, and William was placed in charge of Swarthmore farm, where he continued to reside, suffering attack after attack of acute bronchitis, which developed into rapid consumption, and finally terminated his life in the forty-third year of his age, after a prolonged illness, March 22, 1852. Though in extremely delicate health all his life, rarely free from pain in some form, still he was full of resource, and possessed wonderful energy, united to a remarkably cheerful disposition. He made many and permanent improvements at the old home during the later years of his life. He had many warm friends and acquaintances, and was greatly respected by all classes for his integrity, fair dealing, and many good qualities of head and heart. He was a lovable brother and kind parent, always bore his pains and troubles uncomplainingly, and was tender in his thoughts and feelings for others. Though inheriting a birthright membership in the Society of Friends, it was not until the later years of his life that he took an active and serious interest in its affairs. Confined to his room during the winter months for several years, his heart seemed to go out in loving interest for the spiritual welfare of the many friends who came to see him. Rarely did one leave that room without some word of encouragement or help. His most earnest desire seemed to be that all his relatives and friends might come to know the loving faith which so cheered and sustained those last days of weary suffering and pain.

William Jolliffe was a tall, slender man, over six feet in height, with regular features, good complexion, clear blue eyes, and dark hair, which at his death was so gray as to look almost white. He was neat in dress, very erect in his bearing, and fond of society. His remains were interred at Hopewell Burying-Ground. His wife survived him fourteen years.

Family Record of Joseph Neill Jolliffe and Sarah Janney, his wife. Married 1843.

Joseph Neill Jolliffe, sixth child of William Jolliffe and Rebecca Neill, his wife, was born at Swarthmore farm, Frederick County, Virginia, April 10, 1813. He received his education in the private schools of the county and early began farming, which business he has followed all his life. He has been a great reader of books and papers, and has always kept himself fully posted regarding the topics of the day, possessing clear, well-defined convictions upon all the religious and political problems of the day. When a young man he took charge of his mother's farm near the Burnt Factory, in Clarke County, Virginia. This was a good property of about two hundred and fifty acres, a part of the original Neill homestead. When thirty years of age, on February 14, 1843, he married Sarah Elizabeth Janney (born February 14, 1821), a daughter of George and Susanna (Boone) Janney, of Loudoun County, Virginia. They have had eight children, as follows: Susan Boone;[1] Rebecca Neill, born July 3, 1846, died August 27, 1857; Sarah Sands, born October 10, 1848, died September 25, 1864; Joseph John, born October 10, 1851; Alice Brooks, born January 9, 1854, died November 10, 1854; George Janney, born October 16, 1857; Rachel Williams; and Townsend Sharpless, born September 29, 1864.

---

[1] "George Boone, the grandfather of Daniel Boone, the great hunter and pioneer of the West, immigrated with his wife and eleven children from Exeter, England, in 1717; settled on the banks of the Delaware, where he purchased a tract of land. His son, Squire Boone, was married to Sarah Morgan in September, 1720. He died in Bucks County, Pennsylvania, December, 1743, leaving sons Ralph, Joseph, Solomon, and a daughter Elizabeth. His son Daniel, the great pioneer, was born October 28, 1734, and when about ten years of age removed with his family to near Reading, Bucks County, Pennsylvania, then a frontier settlement; a few years later they moved to North Carolina." One of the great-grandsons of the above George Boone (and probably a grandson of Squire Boone) was Isaiah Boone, who moved to Loudoun County, Virginia. His wife was Susanna Boone. They had among other children a daughter, Susanna Boone, who married George Janney, of Loudoun County, and had three sons and four daughters, one of whom, Sarah Elizabeth Janney, married February 14, 1843, Joseph N. Jolliffe, of Frederick County, Virginia.

After his marriage, Joseph Jolliffe continued to reside in Clarke County until after the death of his brother William, when he moved with his family to the old homestead, Swarthmore (his mother being old he came to look after her interests), and he has ever made this his home.

During the John Brown raid that part of the country was greatly agitated. Joseph Jolliffe took a deep interest in and studied the movement very closely. A few years later and the mutterings of the great Civil War were heard. Few men saw more clearly than he did the inevitable result of such a contest. A firm and consistent Union man, he dared voice his sentiments at the polls, casting the only ballot Abraham Lincoln received in the county of Frederick. When the war actually began he was past the age rendering him liable to military service, and being a consistent Friend he preserved a strictly neutral attitude, but never for one moment changed his strong Union sentiments. He aided the sick and wounded of both armies so far as it was possible for him to do so. He suffered terribly by the war. Having a great deal of valuable timber land, thousands of axes were often going all day long in it, and as this part of the country was a battle-ground from the beginning to the end of the war, it was pretty much all destroyed. His place was pulled to pieces, fencing burned up, implements destroyed, horses and valuable stock, of which he had an abundance, were driven off, and then his business was almost completely suspended for four years. Twice officers were quartered upon him, using his house as head-quarters for a long time, among them being the celebrated General John C. Breckenridge, of Kentucky. Armies were continually passing, and once, September 19, 1864 (Sheridan's battle of Winchester), a sharp engagement was carried on right over the house, some of the bullets, shells, and canister-shot striking the back porch and knocking bricks off the chimneys. The family was advised to take refuge in the cellar, but his daughter and other members of the family lay ill of diphtheria (brought there by the army) at the time, and fearing to risk their lives by taking them into the cellar, they sat through it all by the bedside of the sick, trusting to their heavenly Father's care for protection. The very dogs were so frightened it was hard to get them out of the house after the engagement was all over. They were often reduced to such straits that they scarcely knew where their next supply of food was to come from. Often sick, with no medical aid save that which could be secured from some passing army surgeon, and often many months cut off from communication with their relatives and friends outside of the lines. Once he had to leave his home and with others take refuge with his cousin, Elizabeth S. Hopkins, of Sandy Spring, Maryland, who hospitably sheltered many of her relatives and friends for weeks and months during these times. They have often spoken of how they enjoyed Joseph Jolliffe's visit and his thrilling accounts of scenes and incidents of the war. Once he was arrested and taken ten or twelve miles below his home before General Jubal Early, ostensibly on the excuse of being wanted to pilot his army below Brucetown, but really because General Early had been informed that he was a dangerous man to leave at large. It resulted in their sitting down together under a tree and talking over the situation. General Early, himself having been an ardent Union man before hostilities began (while attending the famous convention in Richmond he came near being mobbed for his bold and fearless opposition to the States being put out of the Union), was the better able to understand Joseph Jolliffe's views. The conversation was spicy and amusing in the extreme, causing Early's staff and other officers to gather around to listen. To General Early's credit the interview resulted in his letting his prisoner return peaceably to his home.

As the war progressed their sufferings were so great that the citizens of the community, united by a common trouble, aided each other irrespective of their parties, whether Union or Confederate, and on one occasion when his cousin, Edward Jolliffe, had been arrested by the Union army, Joseph Jolliffe went with Edward's wife, Virginia Jolliffe, to Martinsburg to try to procure his release. They were suddenly surrounded by members of the celebrated Colonel Mosby's command, were stopped and made to accompany them to the heart of a deep wood some distance from the main road. Here they were kept closely guarded all night long; in the morning they were told they could go on their way unmolested. That night the Baltimore and Ohio Railroad was raided by Mosby's command, a passenger train held up and much valuable booty secured by the Confederates. As the soldiers hurried them off to the woods, our cousin, Virginia Jolliffe, was much alarmed, and kept calling out, "Soldiers, are you going to kill us?" to which reply would be made, "No, madam, we won't kill you." At the close of the war Joseph Jolliffe bought for a few dollars some United States condemned horses and began trying to repair damages. It was slow work, but nature, always kind, in time hid the scars of war, and the land brought forth good crops. The old farm still smiles upon the efforts of his sons and yields them a fair living.

His daughter, Susan B., married Lewis N. Hoge, of Loudoun County, Virginia;[1] for some years they made their home in Clarke County, but moved to North Carolina with their children, one of whom is married. Joseph John married Sarah Lupton, a daughter of Joel Lupton, of Frederick County;[2] they built a home on the

---

[1] William Hoge, born in Scotland, came to America in 1683; married Barbara Hume, settled in New Jersey, moved to Delaware, and in 1735 moved to Frederick County, Virginia, and settled near where Kernstown now is.

William Hoge, eldest son of William and Barbara Hoge, was born at Perth Amboy, New Jersey, and moved to Virginia with his wife Esther and his parents. He joined the Society of Friends and moved with his family to Loudoun County, Virginia. His son, William Hoge, Jr., married July 16, 1795, Rachel Steel. He was disowned by Friends, 1777, for enlisting in the army. Had also sons John and Israel.

James Hoge was son of William Hoge, and grandson of William and Barbara Hoge. He was a Friend, and resided in Loudoun County, Virginia.

Isaac Hoge was the son of James Hoge, of Loudoun County, Virginia. He married Rachel Schofield, daughter of Mahlon and Ann (Neill) Scofield. They had children,—

James Hoge, of Washington, District of Columbia; has a family.

Isaac Hoge, of Loudoun County, Virginia; has a family.

Josephine Hoge, married Lewis N. Hopkins, and left one daughter, Josephine, who died a young lady.

Lewis Neill Hoge, married Susan Boone Jolliffe; is living in North Carolina, and has a family.

William Hoge, of Washington, District of Columbia; has a family.

Annie Hoge, who married Owen Holmes and has one child.

Lewis N. Hoge and Susan B., his wife, have children, James H., Sarah J., Lewis N., and Elizabeth S.

[2] Joseph Lupton, a member of the Society of Friends, came to America from England and first settled in Pennsylvania. He removed to the valley of Virginia about the year 1741, bringing his wife and eight children with him; he was then about fifty years of age, and was born about 1690. His sons were Joseph, ——, David, Joshua, John.

John Lupton, fifth child of Joseph, was born 1725; was fifteen years old when he came to Virginia; was married at Hopewell Meeting-House, Virginia, June 6, 1755, to Sarah Frost, daughter of John Frost, of Virginia, and had seven children. After the death of his first wife he married Ann Rees, widow of Henry Rees (Ann Neill), and daughter of Lewis Neill and Lydia Hollingsworth, his wife, June 13, 1776, at Hopewell Meeting-House, Virginia. They had children, Elizabeth and Jonah.

Elizabeth (Neill) Lupton married Joseph Carter, and was the mother of Lydia Ann, Sarah Elizabeth, Mary Margaret (who died an infant), and Joshua Lupton (who died October, 1887). Elizabeth died 1853.

Joseph Lupton, eldest son of Joseph Lupton (who came to Virginia in 1741), was married to Rachel Bull, daughter of Richard Bull, of Chester County,

old place at the Rock Spring, where with their four sons and one daughter they reside. George J. Jolliffe married Charlotte Huck, a daughter of Richard Huck, of Frederick County[1] (a distant cousin); they with their two sons live near Kernstown (Neill's Mill), Virginia. His daughter, Rachel W. Jolliffe, married Arthur Robinson, of Frederick County,[2] and with their two little children,

---

Pennsylvania, August 17, 1750, at Hopewell Meeting-House, Frederick County, Virginia. They had children, one of whom was David Lupton.

David Lupton, son of Joseph and Rachel (Bull), was married to Mary Hollingsworth, daughter of Isaac (deceased) and Rachel Hollingsworth, June 12, 1777, at Hopewell Meeting-House, Frederick County, Virginia.

Joel Lupton, son of David and Mary (Hollingsworth) Lupton, was married to Sarah G——, at Hopewell Meeting-House, Frederick County, Virginia. Their daughter, Sarah Lupton, was married at Hopewell Meeting-House, October 7, 1875, to Joseph John Jolliffe. Their children are Walker Neill, born July 17, 1876; Joel Lupton, born October 28, 1877; Edith M , born September 2, 1879; and John, born August 9, 1882.

[1] Thomas Huck (was, I believe, at one time an officer in the British army and a Royalist) married Mary Neill, daughter of Joseph Neill and Rebecca McPherson, of Frederick County, Virginia. (Joseph Neill, youngest son of Lewis Neill and Lydia Hollingsworth, his wife, was born November 22, 1757, and was married to Rebecca, daughter of Daniel McPherson, at Hopewell Meeting-House, Virginia, April 7, 1790.) They had three children: (1) Richard Huck, who married Mary Stabler, of Alexandria, Virginia, daughter of —— Stabler and —— Saunders, his wife, who was the daughter of John Saunders, of Alexandria, Virginia. "John Saunders, of Alexandria, son of Joseph and Hannah Saunders, of Philadelphia, to Mary Pancoast, daughter of David and Sarah Pancoast, of Winchester, April 9, 1783." (2) Lewis Neill Huck, of Winchester, Virginia, who married Eliza C. Jones, of Mobile, Alabama. They have no children. (3) Mary Huck, who died a single lady in Winchester, Virginia.

Mary Neill Huck, the mother, died at Swarthmore farm, while on a visit about the year 1850.

Richard Huck had children, Saunders, Hally, Charlotte (Jolliffe), Lewis N. (deceased), Lylly, and Richard.

Charlotte Huck married George J. Jolliffe; their children are Richard H. and Lewis N.

[2] James Robinson was born in Ireland, and married Mary, also born in Ireland, daughter of George Brown. They moved to the valley of Virginia and settled four miles west of White Hall, Frederick County, Virginia.

Andrew A. Robinson, son of James and Mary Robinson, was born in Frederick County, Virginia, in 1781, and died May 7, 1855. He married Margaret Jackson, daughter of Josiah and Ruth (Steer) Jackson, formerly of Chester County, Pennsylvania. They had children, Archibald, Jackson, James, Jonathan, Mary Jane, David, Josiah, Joseph, Margaret A., Andrew A., and William.

Jonathan Robinson, son of Andrew A. Robinson and Margaret Jackson,

live at the "old Severs place," near Hopewell, Virginia. The youngest son, Townsend S. Jolliffe, lives with his parents in the old house, Swarthmore. He is not married and cares for the old couple.

Joseph N. Jolliffe was always respected by his neighbors for his courage and honest convictions, which he lived up to. His relatives and friends love him and honor him for his kindness of heart and sweet disposition. Until recent years he could be seen regularly walking to the railroad station each afternoon except Sunday, when his steps were turned to old Hopewell Meeting-House. Though a very old man, he is one of the most interesting, telling with a quiet humor the many and varied amusing and interesting experiences of himself and friends during war times.

---

married Mary Frances ——; their son, Arthur Robinson, married ——, at Hopewell Meeting-House, Frederick County, Virginia, Rachel Williams Jolliffe, daughter of Joseph N. and Sarah E. Jolliffe, and have children, Sarah Elizabeth and Albert Jolliffe.

Elizabeth A. Jolliffe, fourth child of William Jolliffe and Mary Ann Branham, his wife, was called after her aunt Elizabeth Jolliffe Sharpless, who adopted her on the death of her father in her ninth year. After her aunt's marriage with Townsend Sharpless, of Philadelphia, she went to live with her, and finished her education in that city. She continued to live with her aunt until the death of that lady on March 16, 1883.

William Jolliffe and Emma Randolph Parry, his wife. Married November 26, 1873.

[A friend has prepared the following brief sketch of the life and work of William Jolliffe, civil and mining engineer, at the special request of his wife and children.]

William Jolliffe, sixth child and only living son of William Jolliffe and Mary Ann Branham, his wife, was born at Swarthmore farm, Frederick County, Virginia, June 23, 1847. When but four years old his father died. He early attended the private country schools of the county, and when twelve years of age was sent to Westtown Boarding-School, in Pennsylvania. This was at the time when the war had fairly opened. Harper's Ferry was in possession of the Confederate forces, the bridges between Philadelphia and Baltimore had been burned, and the Relay House was strongly fortified by Federal troops. To pass through these barriers when feeling was running so high was no easy task, and consequently visits to his home by the young lad were attended with considerable danger. He was searched at Harper's Ferry by the Confederate forces and at the Relay House by Federal troops, and was put on a boat at Baltimore, which was guarded by troops until it landed at Havre de Grace, Maryland, where he took the cars for Philadelphia.

For a long time he was cut off from all communication with his mother, but finally succeeded in getting home for a short visit. As the war dragged along these same conditions continued. After Westtown, William Jolliffe attended school for a short time at Union Springs, New York, and in Philadelphia. He was then placed in Sharpless Brothers' large dry-goods store, in Philadelphia, to learn the business, and he remained with that firm for three years. At that time his health failed him, and he was compelled to seek out-door employment. He entered the Polytechnic College of Pennsylvania, in Philadelphia, and studied mining engineering, graduating July 1, 1868, when just twenty-one years of age. He then took a special course in chemistry under Professor Williams, of Philadelphia, where he met George A. Koenig and Preston M. Bruner, both recent graduates of Heidelberg, Germany. While experimenting with waste tin-scrap, these three students discovered a process for utilizing the tin on this waste. Forming the partner-

WILLIAM JOLLIFFE.

ship of Koenig, Bruner & Jolliffe, they took out patents for the manufacture of the salts of tin from tinners' waste, and also for utilizing the iron thus freed from combination, and for the machinery needed in these processes. They erected a factory, working at it themselves, and persevered in further labor upon their invention until it was entirely successful.

However, as is often done in such cases, a combination was formed against them by the large chemical manufacturing establishments of Philadelphia, which speedily forced them out of business. Koenig soon after became a professor in the University of Pennsylvania, and Bruner went to the Bethlehem Steel-Works.

William Jolliffe, making use of his collegiate training, obtained an appointment as draughtsman for the Western Land Association of Minnesota, and went to Duluth. After laying out and mapping a large part of that growing town, he received an appointment in 1870 as resident engineer on the Northern Pacific Railroad, and filled this position until the winter of 1871–72. At that time Mr. Jolliffe received an appointment as chief of a locating party on the Valley Branch of the Baltimore and Ohio Railroad in Virginia. Work being suspended on this line in October, 1872, he went as division engineer on the Atlantic and Great Western Railroad, at Meadville, Pennsylvania, for a short time. Receiving a call as assistant engineer for the city of Pittsburg the winter of 1872–73, he accepted and was there engaged until taken ill with throat trouble aggravated by the smoke and gas of that city. He left Pittsburg and accepted a position as draughtsman for Allison & Sons' large car-works in Philadelphia, where he remained until the panic of 1873.

During his stay in Philadelphia he made his home with his aunt, Elizabeth J. Sharpless. Here he met Emma Randolph Parry, tenth child of Oliver Parry and Rachel Randolph, his wife, and married her November 26, 1873, at the Friends' Twelfth Street Meeting-House, in Philadelphia. They moved to Buchanan, Virginia, where they made their home. They had children, William Parry Jolliffe, born August 29, 1874; Parry Jolliffe, born October 25, 1877, died in Philadelphia, February 26, 1879, and buried at Solebury, Bucks County, Pennsylvania; Elizabeth Neill Jolliffe, born December 30, 1880.

The next position filled by William Jolliffe was that of division engineer on the Valley Branch of the Baltimore and Ohio Railroad in Virginia, in which he continued until the spring of 1874, when work was finally suspended.

In 1875 and 1876 he built a brick house one mile south of Buchanan, which his family occupied as their home. In 1875 he contracted to build Dam No. 5, at Brownstown, West Virginia, for the United States government, being engaged in this work under the firm-name of Schultz & Jolliffe, from which he afterwards retired.

Having conceived the idea of building a railroad from Clifton Forge, Virginia, on the Chesapeake and Ohio Railroad, to Buchanan, Virginia, on the James River and Kanawha Canal, he labored for more than two years to bring this about, assisting in obtaining from the Virginia Assembly a charter. The company was finally organized, work begun, and William Jolliffe appointed chief engineer. When the road was about three-fourths completed, a tremeudous freshet visited the James River Valley, November 22, 1877, and washed away more than half of the new road-bed and damaged the canal to the extent of five hundred thousand dollars. It being absolutely necessary to at once repair the canal, and being the most available man for the position, William Jolliffe was appointed chief assistant engineer of the James River and Kanawha Canal, and with his railroad forces repaired the damages between Richmond and Lynchburg in the winter of 1877–78, opening that watercourse for navigation in March, 1878. Then joining as junior partner the firm of Jordan, Ballard & Co., he was engaged in repairing the canal from Lynchburg to Lexington and Buchanan, which work was pushed with vigor.

On September 12, 1878, a second freshet damaged this new work to the extent of sixty thousand dollars. An extension of time being granted the firm, Jordan, Ballard & Co., again began the work of repair, and completed it in the winter of 1880. The workmen were at once turned back on the road-bed of the Buchanan and Clifton Forge Railroad under William Jolliffe as chief engineer. That winter the Assembly chartered the Richmond and Alleghany Railroad, which bought out the Canal and the Buchanan and Clifton Forge Railroad. William Jolliffe was appointed division engineer on the new road, which place he held for a short time only, ill health, brought on by exposure during the trying times while directing the canal repairs, forcing him to resign. At the thirty-first meeting of the American Institute of Mining Engineers, held at Staunton, Virginia, May 18, 1881, William Jolliffe was elected a member. He was also elected a member of the Association of Engineers of Virginia upon the organization of that body at Roanoke, Virginia, in 1890.

In 1880, William Jolliffe joined the firm of Dillon, Jolliffe & Co., and completed, as contractor, ten miles of heavy work on the Shenandoah Valley Railroad below Buchanan. In 1887 they completed twelve miles of the New River Branch of the Norfolk and Western Railroad. He also joined the firm of Jolliffe & Carpenter and completed in 1881–82 the tunnels and railroad-yards for the Norfolk and Western Railroad at Pocahontas, Virginia. In 1882 he sold his house to the Shenandoah Valley Railroad in Buchanan and moved to Lexington, Virginia, where he resided for four years. In 1883–84 he was manager of the Lexington Manufacturing Company, erecting the buildings, putting in the machinery, and starting the work. In 1885–86 he joined A. D. Estill as a partner, and ran the Beechenbrook Foundry and Machine-Shops in Lexington. This venture did not prove successful, and the firm dissolved. In 1886 he bought at public sale the large farm of four hundred and sixty-four acres, one mile west of Buchanan, Virginia. Remodelling the dwelling-house on the premises, he moved his family to this property, where they have since resided. In 1887 he made a horseback survey for the Virginia Western Railroad in Southwestern Virginia and in Tennessee. In 1888–89 he became division engineer on the Georgia Pacific Railroad at West Point, Mississippi. In the autumn of 1889 he again did work for the Virginia Western Railroad as engineer in charge of surveys. In 1890 he was made chief engineer for the Central Land Company of Buchanan, to which corporation he sold his farm, reserving his dwelling-house and sixty-eight acres of land. Since then he has been in ill health brought on by constant exposure in all sorts of weather while engaged in railroad and other out-door work. He has written various reports on the railroads and mineral resources of the James River Valley, etc. Since graduating, he has constructed or superintended as engineer work aggregating in value four million five hundred thousand dollars, besides making various surveys, estimates, and plans, or at the rate of two hundred thousand dollars per year.

CPSIA information can be obtained
at www.ICGtesting.com
Printed in the USA
LVHW052207280119
605595LV00037B/728/P

9 781333 775650